A LONG WAY FROM TIBET

CARLO BULDRINI

Translated from the Italian by Lakshmi Ramakrishnan Iyer

tara-india research press

tara-india research press
B-4/22, Safdarjung Enclave,
New Delhi – 110 029.
Ph.: 24694610; Fax : 24618737
bahrisons@vsnl.com
contact@indiaresearchpress.com
www.indiaresearchpress.com

Carlo Buldrini, 2005 © India Research Press

ISBN : 81-87943-74-2

All rights reserved by publisher. No part of this publication unless used for Research and Documentation, may be reproduced, stored in or introduced into a retrieval system or transmitted in any form, or by any means, electronic, mechanical, photocopying, recording or otherwise, without the prior written permission of the publisher of this book.

A LONG WAY FROM TIBET
Carlo Buldrini,
Translated by Lakshmi Ramakrishnan Iyer

Cataloguing in Publication Data
Includes bibliographical references.
1. Tibet 2. Travel 3. Dharamsala 4. History
I. Title   II. Author.

Printed in India at Focus Impressions, New Delhi – 110 003.

A LONG WAY
FROM TIBET

To Dekyi

ཕྱིའི་རྡོ་ཅིག་ཞིགས་ཀྱང༌། །ནང་ཆོས་ཅིག་མི་ཞིགས། །

The outside wall of stone can be demolished
But not the inner wall of Dharma.

Tibetan proverb

Prologue

Lhasa, Tibet, China.

A van crawls at a snail's pace along the Beijing Donglu-East Peking Road, the eastern stretch of the road that goes all the way across the city. A large strip of red cloth with hand-drawn Chinese characters on it is wrapped around the van.

A red flag with five stars flutters in the driver's window.

The notes of a military march crackle from a loudspeaker, alternating with a strident female voice shouting, 'Throwing explosive devices, violence, sabotage and theft will be severely punished.'

Around here, 'severely' means 'the death penalty'.

An olive-green Dong Feng military truck moves slowly forward behind the van. The front of the truck is squashed, like the muzzle of a bulldog.

Six Tibetans in chains stand in the back of the truck, guarded by a few members of the People's Armed Police.

The policemen are very young. Their faces are tense. They shoulder machine guns.

The Communist Party Committee of Lhasa's Public Security Bureau has recently launched an anti-crime campaign. The campaign is called 'Strike hard'.

In an article published in *Xizang Ribao* (Tibet Daily), the Lhasa police chief Luobu Dunzhu (Norbu Dhondup) is quoted as saying that 'turning the screw' is meant to 'maintain political stability and social peace.' Norbu says 'acts of sabotage now take place not only in the city but in the countryside as well. Separatist group activity is intensifying.'

Most of the shops in Beijing Donglu are Chinese-owned. Ramrod-straight dummies with blonde hair and a plastic expression wear 'Shingbaolu' men's jackets. A shoeshop sells

'Ya Shi Nan' brand footwear. The next shop sells handbags, women's waistcoats and mini-skirts, all in black leather. The salesgirls are wearing five-inch platform heels.

There is a cosmetics shop that also sells brassières. The salesgirls have copper-coloured hair.

There is a shop selling army uniforms. Two Chinese men are loading thirty-odd caps with a red star on the peak onto a rickshaw.

There is a shop selling kitsch. It has little windmills in bell jars. The window display includes animal-shaped pendulum clocks made of plastic. A black owl with an oscillating tail and eyes that move. Dogs. Cats. A rabbit with a carrot dangling under his nose.

There is a porn shop. Inflatable dolls with red nipples. Condoms with studs on them. Red and black women's panties, hung on the wall on a cellophane-wrapped white cardboard sheet, looking like small kites. The shop's current customers are a young Chinese couple. The woman bends over the condoms displayed in a glass-topped case under the counter.

The van with the red cloth strip and the army truck have covered most of the Beijing Donglu.

The Chinese shops give way to little Tibetan restaurants.

The tiny window of one tavern has an aluminium bowl full of steamed momos. There is also a jar with roasted watermelon seeds.

On the pavement, an elderly Tibetan man is selling colourful posters. Some of them show the Potala, once the residence of the Dalai Lama. Others have Alpine chalets with piebald cows in the forefront.

The van with the red cloth strip and the loudspeaker come up to where the old man is selling his coloured posters.

All of a sudden, a young Tibetan darts out of a side road.

He has long hair gathered into a chignon.

The youth raises his right fist towards the sky. He yells, 'Independence for Tibet', 'Long live His Holiness the Dalai Lama' and 'Chinese, get out of Tibet.'

The van's occupants don't seem to have noticed anything. It moves on.

But the army truck stops. A man leans out of the window. He looks around.

The passers-by—all Tibetans in this part of the city— stop too. They stand still, holding their breath. They look at the men of the People's Armed Police who hold their machine guns at the ready.

But there is no trace of the young Tibetan.

Moments later, the olive-green Dong Feng truck starts moving once again. It accelerates to catch up with the ribbon-tied van that has out-distanced it by almost forty metres.

McLeod Ganj

Dharamsala's bus station was located on the outskirts of the town. A long staircase of reinforced concrete led down to it. The staircase wound, snakelike, along a steep escarpment. There was a beggar every twenty steps.

'Hé babu. Paise, paise.' Three children held out their hands from under a mud-coloured cloth. They looked like three little trained monkeys.

On the front of the big building was written, in block letters: INTER STATE BUS STAND DHARAMSALA.

The bus station had been built recently but was already a wreck. The plastic seats in the entry hall were discoloured and dusty. There was never anyone at the two small stands with the 'Enquiry' sign. Hundreds of sparrows had built their nests in the interstices of the bricks. At four in the afternoon their twittering was deafening.

Groups of passengers were waiting. Sikh soldiers in camouflage gear and olive green turbans. Young honeymooning Indian couples. Tibetans.

Things started getting very animated under the platform roof as a departure got underway. The conductor was shouting out the name of the place to which the bus was going. 'Palampur. Palampur. Palampur.'

The roar of the engine accelerated. The stink of the exhaust pipe began filling the air. The passengers who had arrived late were screaming at the driver to wait.

The buses to McLeod Ganj left from the furthest lane. It was only a nine-kilometre run. The passengers were nearly all Tibetans.

An elderly woman with a sun-burned face smiled at me. She was wearing a blue 'Dallas Cowboys' cap. Two heavy turquoise stones in a solid gold frame hung from her earlobes.

The elderly Tibetan woman had a lot of luggage. She asked me if I could help her to get it on the bus. She indicated a heavy cloth bag and placed a transparent plastic bag in my hand.

The bag held spinach, carrots, ginger and a cauliflower. I found her a place in the first row behind the driver. She thanked me with another smile. With a movement of her hand she indicated the seat next to her. I would have to help her get off the bus too.

More Tibetan women got on, laughing and talking animatedly. They wore the traditional 'chuba' and, over it, the 'pagden,' an apron with thin horizontal stripes.

A young travelling salesman pushed his way with some difficulty along the corridor of the bus. He was selling a small book titled *Perfect English Speaking*. It cost fifteen rupees and had a colourful cover. No one bought a copy.

The driver climbed in through a door next to his seat. He had dyed hair and a thin moustache. The glass panel behind him had 'Kaam ki puja hai' (work is worship) on it in Hindi, as well as the mystic syllable 'Om'.

We left.

The bus had a very shrill horn.

We proceeded slowly. In Kotwali Bazaar the traffic was alternately one-way. Drivers argued over right of way.

Immediately outside Dharamsala the road began to climb. The air got cooler. We crossed woods of pine and Himalayan oak. The trees wore their late autumn colours.

The conductor arrived. The cost of the entire trip from Dharmasala to McLeod Ganj was six rupees.

Several passengers got down at the Cantonment, the army headquarters. Others got on, and the bus remained as crammed as before. With each bump it seemed ready to split into two.

At five in the afternoon Forsyth Ganj was large sleepy. The bus stopped in front of a photography store, 'Kailash Studio'. It left again in a few minutes.

The mountain peaks on the horizon were covered by thin, dark fog.

An old Gothic church appeared unexpectedly. Several ancient tombs surrounded it. The tombs looked like badly washed laundry laid out on the grass to dry.

A line of black-and-yellow three wheelers was parked on the side of the road. Three red-bottomed macaques were tightrope-walking a green-painted iron railing.

A sign read 'Welcome to McLeod Ganj, India's Little Lhasa.'

The main square of McLeod Ganj was teeming with people.

There were coolies with black belts over their shoulders, which they used to fasten their loads on to their backs. The porters had thin faces, jet-black hair and unshaved beards. They waited for customers, standing motionless like shepherds in some ancient nativity scene.

There were old hippies well past fifty with grey hair and a melancholy look about them. Tibetan women walked past rapidly, their children hanging on to them. There were droves of guffawing Indian tourists.

A small black cow had stopped in the middle of the road. A thread of spittle hung from its mouth. Two stray dogs were lapping at the murky water in a sewer. Groups of monks observed the goings-on silently.

Across the dull crowd at McLeod Ganj Bus Stand I met the gaze of a young woman. She had remarkably lovely blue eyes. Her name was Helene. She was seventeen years old. She was from Germany.

Helene had hair cropped as short as a boy's and an angelic face. Rudolf, her boyfriend, was two years older than she was. He wore his hair long, flowing over his shoulders.

Rudolf had a small rucksack slung over his chest.

Out of the black rucksack peered the frightened face of a puppy.

The two youngsters pulled him out very carefully. 'We found him in Pathankot,' they told me. 'We're looking after him. He had a broken leg.'

Helene and Rudolf had been living in McLeod Ganj for two months. They would remain there until their visas expired.

'Why only here?' I asked.

'We're Buddhists,' they replied.

Early next morning I went to the neo-Gothic church at Forsyth Ganj.

The road crossed large pine forests populated by packs of monkeys.

The door of the church was bolted shut. There was an old photocopied notice pasted on a column. It said 'Carols by candle light on 24th December at 6 p.m. Please bring your own candles.' The notice was signed Rev. K. J. Kunjumon.

There was a cemetery behind the Anglican church. It had a large, mock-Gothic funeral monument made of grey stone and topped with a white cross. It was dedicated to Lord Elgin, eighth Viceroy of India.

On the tombstone was written:

IN MEMORY OF
JAMES BRUCE,
EARL OF ELGIN AND KINCARDINE
VICEROY AND GOVERNOR GENERAL
OF INDIA
WHO DIED IN DHURMSALA

IN THE DISCHARGE OF HIS DUTIES,
ON THE 20TH NOVEMBER 1863
AGED 52 YEARS AND 4 MONTHS.

Before he came here to Dharamsala to die, the eighth Viceroy of India had also been Governor of Jamaica and Canada and British ambassador to China. He had had a brilliant career.

I returned to McLeod Ganj.

Two-storeyed buildings flanked three sides of the bus station square. They held bars and restaurants. To the south was the 'Mc'llo Beer Bar & Restaurant', where you could eat masala dosa and listen to old Beatles songs. To the east was 'Hot Spot'—tea, warm lemonade, apple pie and carrot cake. To the north was 'Holiday Snacks'. A sign with painted letters advertised its specialities—'Chowmien. Italiyan Food. Indian Thali.'

A long building just one floor high closed off the western side of the square. It had a sloping roof covered with a layer of tar paper. Three pointed dormer windows stuck out from the roof. Under the one in the centre was a shop sign:

ESTD. 1860
NOWROJEE & SON
GENERAL MERCHANTS
HOUSE & ESTATE AGENTS AUCTIONEERS
MANUFACTURERS
HIGHCLASS MINERAL WATERS.

I went in.

An uneven wooden surface underfoot passed for a floor. The place was dimly lit. There were only two neon lights for the entire—very large—room. A petroleum lamp also hung from the ceiling. It hadn't been used since Mahatma Gandhi's time.

There were several small display cases along the walls. The room was furnished with thin-legged teak furniture.

There were old poster advertisements all over the place.

A fat major domo wearing a red uniform and a wig advertised Cinzano. A woman from the 1930s advertised Pears soap. A young woman in a flyaway dress sat astride a fiery red bull in a poster advertising Dewars White Label Whisky.

Madeleine Carroll, 'the beautiful British Star,' smiled out of a sepia photograph. Her lips were painted. She was advertising State Express Cigarettes 333. The cigarettes were packed in slim tin boxes. 'Luxury cigarettes at an inexpensive price,' read the slogan.

Another young woman was seated on an Eastern-style cushion, holding a box of 'Havinden's Chocolate' in her lap.

In one corner of the shop there was a bottle of beer almost one metre high. 'Beck's. Produce of Germany' was written on the dusty label.

There were three signboards hung on the wall: 'ANDREWS LIVER SALT AND KEEP FIT', 'FIRST WITH THE NEWS. THE TRIBUNE', 'J.B. MANGHARAM & CO'S FAMOUS BISCUITS SOLD HERE'.

When I visited it, Nowrojee & Son only sold newspapers, toffees, detergent, toothpaste, disinfectant, shoe polish and candles.

At the shop entrance there were three small round tables stacked one on top of the other. On the tables were glass jars filled with toffees.

Through the glass jars I spotted a tiny old lady sitting on a cane chair. Her hair was white and freshly permed. A spider's web of wrinkles criss-crossed her face. A single tooth emerged from her gums. She held a hot water bottle on her knees. Behind the old lady was a large gold-framed mirror. The glass was totally oxidised. The shop's rare customers appeared and vanished like ghosts from a distant past.

I asked the old lady to tell me the story of this enchanted store.

Mani Nowrojee said she was 'almost eighty'. She lived in McLeod Ganj with her husband, Mr. Nauzer. They were the fifth generation to own Nowrojee & Son.

The lady invited me to sit down on the chair next to hers.

'We are Zoroastrians,' she said. 'We come from Persia. Ours is a small community scattered throughout Central Asia.

'The shop is as old as McLeod Ganj. It was built in 1860. We used to serve the English soldiers stationed at the Cantonment. Our speciality was fizzy water. It was bottled with the Nowrojee & Son label.

'Little by little, the bungalows of rich Indians—high-ranking officials from Amritsar and Lahore and Muslim nawabs—began to come up alongside those of the English.

'Hindus, Muslims, Gurkhas and Christians all lived here, cheek by jowl, in peace.

'One April morning in 1905 a terrible earthquake destroyed almost the entire area. Nadirshaw Nowrojee, my future father-in-law, was twenty years old at the time. It was five in the morning and he was doing his puja on the veranda of the shop. He had lit a sandalwood fire and was reciting his prayers. All of a sudden, he saw the house in front collapse. He ran into the street and managed to reach safety. The Nowrojees helped people in McLeod Ganj who had been affected by the earthquake. They distributed food, blankets and money.

'In 1914, when my mother-in-law came here to marry, they carried her up in a dandi, a palanquin. It was a whole day's journey from Pathankot to McLeod Ganj. The porters would relieve each other every two hours.

'For another thirty years life in McLeod Ganj went on peacefully. Then we got to 1947 and the Partition. The Muslims had to leave the country. There were few buses and no one wanted to help them to leave. So my husband turned to the English army. The Muslims left with an escort of armed soldiers. No one touched a hair on their heads.

'With Independence the English sold their bungalows and McLeod Ganj became a ghost town. In 1960 my husband came to know that the Indian government was looking for a place to house the Tibetan refugees. He wrote to Prime Minister Jawaharlal Nehru and suggested McLeod Ganj. The proposal was accepted. My husband contacted the owners of the bungalows and houses of McLeod Ganj and convinced them to welcome the Tibetans.

'The bungalow of the District Commissioner was chosen to house the Dalai Lama. The bungalow was called Highcraft House. It was re-named Swargashram.

'The ministers of the Tibetan government in exile, the religious authorities and His Holiness' secretaries often came to see us. Even the Dalai Lama's older sister would come and visit us almost every evening. In the beginning, my husband would meet the Dalai Lama every week.

'Life in McLeod Ganj changed a lot with the arrival of the Tibetans. New houses were built. Foreign tourists started coming. Hotel and shops opened all over the place. Today my husband and I continue to be on good terms with the Dalai Lama. He is a good, kind person. When he laughs, it is from the heart. He is always happy and he wants everyone else to be that way too. The pain he feels about having lost his country is something he keeps exclusively to himself.'

***

It was only a ten-minute walk from the bus station square to Tsuglagkhang. The temple was a nondescript, faded yellow building. The façade consisted of eight circular pillars that held up the two floors of the construction. Two flights of stairs led to the Main Temple on the upper floor.

A wide gallery ran all the way around the shrine. There were sixty-two prayer barrels fitted into the wall. The faithful spun them, murmuring the mantra 'Om mani padme hum.'

In front of the temple entrance, a display case held three chalices filled to the brim with butter. A lighted wick made them burn as a sign of devotion.

The Tsuglagkhang hall was of a modest size. The walls were painted yellow. Leaning against the wall at the far end was a large statue of the Buddha Shakyamuni.

The Buddha had the face of a teenager, with half-closed eyes, fleshy lips and deformed ear lobes. A yellow brocade garment left his right shoulder exposed. The statue was made of shiny bronze.

The Buddha was seated in the lotus position. In his left hand he held a beggar's bowl. With his right hand he touched the earth, calling upon it to witness his enlightenment.

On the altar in front of the Buddha were two glass cups with eight packets of Britannia biscuits on top.

There was a chapel to the left of the altar. A folding metal gate with a lock prevented the visitor access. The inside of the chapel was visible through the wide mesh of the gate.

Two large statues had their eyes turned eastwards in the direction of Tibet.

A sign explained:

> THIS IS THE IMAGE OF
> GURU PADMASMBHAVA,
> A GREAT INDIAN SIDDHA,
> WHO CAME TO TIBET IN THE 8TH CENTURY.

Padmasambhava sat cross-legged. He was frowning and wild-eyed. He had on a metal foil garment. On his head he wore the cap of the Nyingma order.

The Guru had a trident with four skulls skewered onto the staff. In his right hand he held the 'vajira,' the 'unyielding sceptre,' symbol of spiritual power. In his left hand he had a cup carved from a human skull. It contained the nectar of immortality.

There was a display case at the statue's feet. Another sign explained, 'The heads of two ancient statues destroyed in Lhasa in 1966 during the Cultural Revolution.'

The heads looked as if they had been pulled off the bodies of two wizened mummies.

To Padmasambhava's left was a second statue:

> THIS IS THE IMAGE OF
> AVALOKITESHWARA
> BODHISATTVA OF COMPASSION,
> WHO IS THE PATRON DEITY
> OF TIBET.

The statue of Avalokiteshwara, the Boddhisattva of Compassion, had three groups of three heads placed on three superimposed levels. Still higher was the head of Vajrapani. On top of them all was the head of Amitabha. The statue had a total of eleven heads. Avalokiteshwara, 'Chenrezig' to the Tibetans, had a thousand arms, eight in front and nine hundred and ninety-two behind.

The massive silver statue contained pieces of another statue of the Boddhisattva of Compassion. This statue had once been in Lhasa's Jokhang. King Songtsen Gampo had had it made in the seventh century. During the Cultural Revolution the Red Guards smashed it to smithereens. The Tibetans collected and hid the pieces. In 1967 they had smuggled them to McLeod Ganj.

On the ground floor of the Tsuglagkhang a big glass door

closed off a square, garage-like room. Inside it, covered by a yellow brocade cloth, was the throne of the fourteenth Dalai Lama. The next day Tenzin Gyatso, the 'emanation' of Chenrezig, would impart his teaching seated on that throne.

The next morning I woke late. I ran to Tsuglagkhang, still half-asleep. The square in front of the temple was full of devotees. There were several elderly people. They prayed with folded hands or turned their prayer wheels.

The upper floor of the temple was packed with monks. They looked like a lot of red worms on a slab of yellow cheese.

I found a place against the outer wall of the Namgyal monastery. Next to me were a Japanese monk, three elderly German flower children and a very young English couple.

The Dalai Lama arrived, preceded by three elderly monks. Four plainclothes policemen followed him.

Tenzin Gyatso climbed the stairs leading to the throne with quick steps, his body bent forward. The devotees made the three ritual prostrations. From where I stood I could see hundreds of bottoms suspended in mid-air.

The teaching began.

On the programme for the morning was the fourth chapter of Shantideva's *Bodhisattvacharyavatara*. The chapter was titled 'Conscientiousness'.

The Dalai Lama began reading the text in Tibetan in his warm, strong voice. He rocked his body gently back and forth.

'Enemies such as hatred and craving
Have neither arms nor legs
And are neither courageous nor wise;
Why, then, have they made me their slave?

They have their dwelling within my mind,
And do me damage at their whim,

Yet I tolerate them without rebelling,
But this is an unsuitable, shameful time for patience'.

The Dalai Lama's observations came to me in an English translation from the earphone of a small radio. 'Shantideva said that our real enemies are mental afflictions - anger, hate, attachment, jealousy. As long as these enemies remain undisturbed inside us, we will not be able to reach real happiness. We must exercise our minds and develop interior discipline. Only in this way will we succeed in changing our way of seeing things and modifying our behaviour.'

The Dalai Lama started reading again.

'Paragraph 47,' he said.

A gust of wind caused the long, narrow pages of Shantideva's book to flutter away. Two monks rushed to collect them. The Dalai Lama laughed in amusement.

'If these disturbing conceptions are not concrete objects; if they exist neither in our senses, nor between the two, nor elsewhere,
Where, then, do they exist, and how are they capable of harming the world?
They are like an illusion. Thus I should dispel the fear within my heart and strive resolutely towards wisdom.
Why should I suffer the torments of Hell for no real reason?'

It was almost lunchtime. The Dalai Lama was tired.

'It is important that we live a life of constant awareness and mental alertness,' was his final instruction.

In the afternoon I decided not to go to the teachings. Instead I went for a walk along Mall Road.

The road started at the McLeod Ganj bus stand and went through woods of pine, oak and rhododendron. The Dalai Lama's voice could be heard, amplified by loudspeakers, all the way up here. Frequent bouts of coughing made his teachings somewhat painful to hear.

I came across a pack of langur monkeys. They stopped to watch me go by. There was an old male and several females, the smallest of their children clinging to their stomachs. The monkeys had black faces and white down on their heads. Their bodies were grey and round. They had extremely long tails that ended in little white puffs.

The warm sunlight filtered through the branches overhead. There was a magnificent sunset.

In the evening, McLeod Ganj was overrun by Tibetan monks and nuns. They were everywhere — in the shops, in the restaurants, loafing about on the streets.

I went to dinner at the 'Kailash Hotel & Restaurant'.

The place was on the first floor of a building in the Main Bazaar, right in front of a small temple.

A thin cloth curtain separated the hotel and restaurant. A narrow corridor led to the rooms. Beside each door was a line with the washing hung out to dry — underpants, socks, T-shirts, bras.

Suresh, the waiter, gave me a piece of paper on which to write my order: 'Special Noodle Soup. Hot Lemon with Honey and Ginger'.

That evening the restaurant was full. The customers were all Tibetan monks. Another two arrived, and I invited them to sit at my table.

They were both about thirty. Only Yeshi could speak a little English. His friend Tenzin had a deep voice and ears that stuck out. He was very shy.

Yeshi ordered a Fanta, Tenzin a Limca.

Yeshi had run away from Tibet in 1989. He had crossed the high Himalayan passes on foot. Since the age of fifteen he had been a monk at Ganden, the fifteenth-century monastery razed to the ground during the Cultural Revolution. Yeshi's family had remained in Tibet. They were peasants. They lived in a small village a two-hour bus ride from the capital.

'Tenzin went through nine months of imprisonment in a Lhasa prison,' his friend told me.

The two monks asked me if I was Buddhist.

'I'm an agnostic,' I replied.

They didn't understand. So I simplified things a bit. 'I'm an atheist,' I said.

'Oh, if you're an atheist, Buddhism is right for you,' Yeshi said with a smile. He added, 'Buddhism is a process of perfecting yourself. The most important thing is compassion. Buddhism is not separate from your life. You can experiment with it in your mind.'

When I came out of the 'Kailash Restaurant', it was already night.

The distant lights of Dharamsala twinkled in the dark like stars fallen from the sky.

The Tenth of March

10th March 1959.

The 'Library of Tibetan Works and Archives' was located halfway between McLeod Ganj and Dharamsala. One reached it by following a rocky path that descended sharply through woods of pine and Himalayan oak.

The Library building was the most beautiful of the entire complex that housed the 'Gangchen Kishong', the Tibetan 'central administration'.

I had gone early in the morning to the Department of Information and International Relations to ask for accreditation for the 10th March demonstration.

I was given a pass with PRESS written on it and the symbol of the Tibetan government in exile.

I had the entire day before me. I decided to go to the library.

The library was on the ground floor of a solid building of reinforced concrete.

The veranda was decorated, Tibetan style, in bright colours. The heads of infernal creatures were painted on the capitals.

Inside, a bronze plaque recalled the names of the two designers:

> THE BUILDING WAS DESIGNED BY
> RAMESH KHOSLA AND KALON J. TARING
> IN THE YEAR 1972.
> THE LIBRARY IS DEDICATED TO THE
> TIMELESS CULTURAL LINKS
> BETWEEN TIBET AND INDIA.

There were wooden benches with foam rubber cushions

on them in the entrance hall. A sign on the wall read: 'No sleeping on the benches'.

I asked for the librarian.

Pema Yeshi was a little over thirty. He wore a striped shirt and a pair of black velvet trousers. His steel-framed glasses with round lenses gave him the look of an intellectual.

'I would like to read something about the revolt in Lhasa in 1959,' I told him.

'It has been written about in many books,' he replied, and invited me to take a seat in the reading room.

In the room, four polygonal pillars held up a pale blue ceiling that was flaking because of the humidity.

There were more signs on the walls. 'Eating, drinking, smoking and sleeping in the Library Reading Room are strictly prohibited.' 'Pets such as dogs, cats and other animals shall not be brought inside the Library'.

Painted on the wall was a large portrait in oils of the Dalai Lama. Tenzin Gyatso was young and smiling. He was leafing through an antique Tibetan text. The artist, Hanna Fiala Ghosh, had dedicated it 'to the people of Tibet.'

From the windows came a suffused light and the murmuring of elderly Tibetans who circled the library reciting mantras and turning their prayer wheels.

Pema Yeshi, the librarian, brought me four books — *The Revolt in Tibet* by Frank Moraes, *My Land and My People* by the Dalai Lama, *From the Land of Lost Content* by Noel Barber and *In Exile from the Land of Snows* by John Avedon.

I immersed myself in the books.

By closing time that evening, I had managed to reconstruct most of the events that had taken place in Lhasa in March 1959.

I wrote down my notes as if they were wire reports.

LHASA, 28th February 1959. Hundreds of refugees continue to

arrive in the Tibetan capital. They come from the eastern provinces of Amdo and Kham. In these regions, armed conflict between the local people and the Chinese People's Liberation Army began five years ago. The Amdovans and Khampas set up mass opposition to the programme of 'democratic reforms' imposed by the Beijing government. The monasteries became the centres of Tibetan resistance. In February 1956, the two monasteries of Changtreng and Lithang, with thousands of civil refugees inside, were bombarded by Chinese warplanes. Over three thousand people died. After these bombardments the Khampa rebellion extended itself to the entire north-eastern part of the country. Mao Zedong's Red Army put it down bloodily. Thousands of Khampa refugees sought shelter in central Tibet.

In Lhasa, provisions and basic essentials have been lacking for months. The number of soldiers belonging to Chinese occupation troops in the capital is estimated to be over 20,000. The number of refugee families who have found shelter in Lhasa and its immediate vicinity is over 15,000.

LHASA, 1st March 1959. In the late morning today two young Chinese army officials went to the Jokhang, the Central Cathedral, and asked to meet the Dalai Lama. In the name of General Tan Guansan, the deputy representative of the Chinese government in Lhasa, they invited Tibet's highest temporal and spiritual authority to attend a theatre performance to be organised in his honour at Silingpu, the headquarters of the Chinese military command. The Dalai Lama accepted the invitation. He reserved the right, however, to fix the date of his attendance at the event only after the exam he was due to take on the 4th March to obtain the 'Geshe Lharampa', the doctorate in metaphysics.

LHASA, 3rd March. The abbot of the Gyume monsatery, consulted the oracle of the Nechung monastery. He asked what could be done in this time of great distress to protect the Dalai Lama, Buddhism and the Tibetan government. The oracle replied: 'Ngekyi lopon thongwa donden di/Phyikye mepai Kulma debre ren', 'It is time to tell the all-knowing Guru not to venture outside.' The prophecy was written on a thick sheet of Tibetan paper to which the seal of the oracle was affixed.

LHASA, 3rd March. Early in the afternoon, Lhasa Radio broadcast the news that the Dalai Lama would attend the meeting of the National Congress of the Chinese People scheduled to take place in Beijing in April. Sources close to the Tibetan government denied the news and defined it as 'completely baseless.'

LHASA, 4th March. Twenty-four-year-old Tenzin Gyatso, the fourteenth Dalai Lama of Tibet, passed the metaphysics doctorate exam with flying colours.

The exam was held at the Lhasa Jokhang in the presence of over ten thousand monks. It was the highlight of the Monlam festival being held in the Tibetan capital for the last ten days.

LHASA, 5th March. The Dalai Lama moved today from the Potala to the Norbulingka, his summer residence. The Norbulingka, the 'jewel-park', is located in the western suburbs of the capital. A multicoloured procession accompanied the Tibetan 'God-King' through two columns of cheering crowds to the Summer Palace. At the head of the parade were three cavalry soldiers dressed in antique Tibetan costumes. They preceded a band playing 'God Save the King'. The Dalai Lama's personal effects followed, transported in the shade of lofty yellow parasols. Then it was the turn of an entire Tibetan army cavalry unit. Then came the high-ranking dignitaries, the old monks and members of Tenzin Gyatso's family. The Tibetan 'God-King' was seated inside a palanquin upholstered in yellow silk. He was carried on the shoulders of thirty-six attendants. At the rear of the procession were the lay authorities in hierarchical order.

For the first time since 1950, the Chinese authorities did not take part in the parade.

LHASA, 7th March. General Tan Guansan has renewed his invitation to the Dalai Lama to attend a theatre performance to be held in his honour at Silingpu, the headquarters of the Chinese Army in Lhasa. The Dalai Lama has accepted the invitation once again and proposed the 10th March as the date of his attendance at the event.

LHASA, 9th March. The Chinese military attaché Brigadier Fu has established the protocol for the Dalai Lama's visit to the military command. Brigadier Fu has specified that no armed personnel should accompany the Dalai Lama and that no soldier is to escort him beyond the Stone Bridge.

According to Depon Tekla, commanding officer of the Dalai Lama's personal guard regiment, the conditions imposed by the Chinese for the visit of Tenzin Gyatso to Silingpu are 'absolutely unacceptable'.

LHASA, 9th March. Surkhang, Liushar and Shasur, three ministers of the kashag, the Tibetan government, have confirmed that the Dalai Lama will be present at the theatre performance scheduled for tomorrow, the 10th March. The Dalai Lama has agreed to go to Silingpu unescorted. The Lhasa police has announced special traffic restrictions on Tuesday 10th March. 'No one will be allowed to go beyond the Stone Bridge,' the order reads.

LHASA, 9th March. Thousands of Tibetans, men, women and children, are assembling outside the outer city walls of the Norbulingka, the Dalai Lama's summer residence. They are shouting slogans—'Tibet for the Tibetans' and 'Free Tibet'. The demonstrators want to stop the Dalai Lama going to Silingpu, the headquarters of the People's Liberation Army. 'The Chinese want to kidnap him and take him to Beijing,' the demonstrators say.

Other protest marches are being held in Lhasa outside the Indian and Nepalese consulates.

LHASA, 10th March. There are now over 30,000 demonstrators

guarding the Norbulingka. Things are extremely tense. In a few hours time the Dalai Lama will have to leave the Summer Palace to go—unescorted—to Chinese army headquarters.

LHASA, 10th March. The demonstrators guarding the Norbulingka since yesterday evening have killed the Tibetan monk, Khunchung Sonam Gyatso, a member of the Religious Affairs Committee of the PCART (Preparatory Committee of the Autonomous Region of Tibet).

Late this morning, Khunchung arrived at the main entry of the Summer Palace on a bicycle. He was wearing a white shirt, a pair of dark trousers, a Chinese hat and a gauze mask as protection against the dust that covered most of his face. At first the demonstrators mistook him for a Chinese and stopped him. Seeing that he was surrounded, the man extracted a revolver hidden in his belt and fired two shots in the air. The people then immobilised him and pushed him to the ground. They stripped off his gauze mask. 'It's that traitor Khunchung,' someone shouted. Khunchung was in fact widely known to be a Chinese collaborator. The demonstrators struck him repeatedly with punches and kicks. The enraged crowd then stoned him to death. The death of Khunchung Sonam Gyatso was long and harrowing. The corpse was dragged, its feet tied, all the way to the Barkor, the sacred circuit that encircles the Jokhang, the Central Cathedral of Lhasa.

LHASA, 10th March. A large demonstration below the Potala by the citizens of Lhasa ended in the early afternoon. The demonstrators shouted anti-Chinese slogans. They loudly demanded 'rangzen,' independence. The orators declared the Seventeen-Point Agreement between the People's Republic of China and the Tibetan government void. The demonstration was organised by activists of the 'Mimang Tsongdu' or People's Assembly, a group of Tibetan militants founded by Alo Chonzed in 1954.

LHASA, 10th March. Tibetan troop movements have been signalled at the headquarters situated in the northern part of the city.

A contingent of two thousand men will leave the headquarters tonight to move south of the Kyichu River. There are increasingly persistent rumours of a possible flight by the Dalai Lama from the Summer Palace. Arms and ammunition have been supplied to all the members of the National Volunteer Defence Army inside the Norbulingka. The volunteer army is also known as 'Chu-zhi Gang-drung'—Four Rivers, Six Rangers, one of the Kham region's old names. This anti-Chinese resistance movement was created by Khampa militants who took refuge in Lhasa and the Lhokha region after their defeat in their own region at the hands of Chinese People's Liberation Army soldiers. Andrug Gonbo Tashi is the leader of the movement.

After having tried in vain to make contact with the Dalai Lama and his government, the American Central Intelligence Agency decided to offer a limited amount of support to the Chu-zhi Gang-drung movement. The CIA supplied the Khampa militants with weapons on two occasions in 1958. Some of them were trained at the American base on the island of Saipan in the Pacific Ocean[1].

LHASA, 10th March. General Tan Guansan declared that, if the Tibetan government did not immediately restore order in the capital, 'drastic measures will be taken to crush opposition to the Chinese regime in Tibet.'

LHASA, 10th March. In reply to a letter from General Tan Guansan, the Dalai Lama has written: 'I sincerely meant to come to the military command to attend the theatre performance. Unfortunately the crowd of lay and religious demonstrators prevented me from doing so. These demonstrators are incited by a small group of ill-intentioned persons. I am deeply sorry about this and, at the

---

1. With Andrug Gonpo Tashi's exile to India on the 28th April 1959, the Four Rivers, Six Rangers movement ceased operations within Tibet. The movement re-formed in the region of Mustang in northern Nepal. In July 1972, after U.S. President Richard Nixon's visit to China, the CIA decided to suspend all support to the Tibetan resistance movement. In a taped message, the Dalai Lama himself asked the Khampa militants operating in Mustang to give up their arms. Many of them committed suicide by slitting their own throats when they heard the Dalai Lama's words.

moment, I find myself unable to move freely.'

LHASA, 12th March. In an unprecedented move, the Dalai Lama has convened sixty leaders of the People's Representative group inside the Norbulingka.

LHASA, 13th March. Tibetan spies report intense military activity by the Chinese army. Twenty heavy cannons have been transported to Lhasa from a small centre twenty kilometres from the capital. Another four cannons and twenty-eight machine guns have been carried to Lhasa from a power station site on the city's outskirts. The Tibetans, in their turn, have responded by erecting barricades at the city's nerve centres. The windows of the Potala have machine gun barrels sticking out of them. Tibetan army soldiers have carried weapons and ammunition to the Iron Hill where the Institute of Tibetan Medicine, now transformed into a military bunker, has its headquarters.

LHASA, 16th March. A third letter from General Tan Guansan to the Dalai Lama. The envelope also contained a letter from Ngabo Ngawang Jigme, a Tibetan government minister who has gone over to the Chinese side. Ngabo wrote to the Dalai Lama: 'If Your Holiness, together with your closest collaborators, stays inside the inner walls of the Norbulingka (the 'yellow walls') and informs General Tan which building you intend to remain in, that building will certainly not be damaged.' Everything seems, therefore, to indicate that the Chinese are getting ready to bombard the Norbulingka.

LHASA, 16th March. Phala, the Dalai Lama's chief of protocol, has issued an order forbidding the use of electric torches at night. Meanwhile, a part of Lhasa's population continues to garrison the Norbulingka.

NEW DELHI, 17th March. Speaking in the Lok Sabha in Delhi, the Indian Prime Minister Jawaharlal Nehru said that the news reaching India of the alleged disorder taking place in Lhasa is nothing but 'bazaar gossip.' Nehru said that Tibet was facing a 'clash of mentalities rather than a clash of armies.' The Indian Prime Minister concluded his speech in Parliament saying, 'there is no large-scale violence happening in that country.'

LHASA, 17th March. At five in the afternoon the Chinese army fired two rounds of mortar on the Norbulingka. The first shell exploded in a small artificial lake inside the walls of the Summer Palace, the second just outside the walls. The three Tibetan government ministers who have taken refuge inside the Norbulingka called the current situation 'the most serious crisis in the history of Tibet.'

LHASA, 17th March. After two explosive devices were set off near the Norbulingka, the kashag (the Tibetan government) and the Dalai Lama separately consulted the Nechung oracle. In both cases the oracle said that remaining inside the Summer Palace no longer offers any guarantee of safety.

LHASA, 17th March. At eight-thirty in the evening the mother of the Dalai Lama left Norbulingka with her eldest daughter and thirteen-year-old son. All three were dressed as Tibetan soldiers.

LHASA, 17th March. At ten in the evening the fourteenth Dalai Lama of Tibet left the Norbulingka secretly.

Tenzin Gyatso was wearing a brown chuba, a fur hat and a woollen scarf that covered most of his face. The Dalai Lama carried a rifle on his shoulders and had taken off his glasses so as not be recognised.

LHASA, 18th March. Chinese troops are being massively deployed along the city's north-south axis. The men of the People's Liberation Army clearly intend to isolate the centre of Lhasa from its western suburb that includes the Potala, the Iron Hill, the Norbulingka and the Indian consulate. Chinese troops are digging trenches along the road that runs in front of the village of Shol at the feet of the Potala. The entire Shuktri Lingka, the large park in front of Shol, has been transformed into a Chinese military base.

LHASA, 18th March. Tibetan Army soldiers are also preparing for the clash. They are armed with rifles, mortar guns and a few items of heavy artillery. The Tibetan soldiers are positioning their old cannons, which are pulled along by mules.

CHE-LA PASS (TIBET), 18th March. At eight-thirty in the morning the Dalai Lama's group, fleeing Lhasa, reached the base of the Che-la Pass. The pass is 5,180 metres high.

LHASA, 18th March. A large demonstration organised by the Women's Association is taking place. The Tibetan women are shouting slogans and carrying banners with the words 'Tibet to the Tibetans.'

RA-ME MONASTERY (TIBET), 18th March. After almost twenty hours of continuous travel, at four-thirty in the afternoon today the Dalai Lama and his followers reached the Ra-Me monastery, where they will spend the night.

LHASA, 20th March. At two in the morning the Chinese army began bombarding the city. The Norbulingka was the first target to be hit. Hundreds of Tibetan civilians died.

LHASA, 20th March. The clashes between Chinese People's Liberation Army soldiers and the people of Lhasa have spread to the entire city. There has been particularly violent combat in the small streets around the Jokhang, the Central Cathedral. The combat is often hand-to-hand. There are numerous victims on both sides.

LHASA, 20th March. The Chinese army has begun bombarding the Iron Hill with its heavy artillery positioned in Shuktri Lingka.

LHASA, 20th March. A violent battle is taking place in Sagyari Street and the small adjoining roads. Tibetan women have built barricades of sandbags and balls of wool in the roads around the Jokhang.

LHASA, 20th March. Lhasa Radio announced that the 'rebels'

have destroyed the portraits of the President Mao Zedong and substituted them with posters that read 'Chinese, go home.' The radio also said that 'the rebels are launching inflammatory slogans against the State.'

LHASA, 20th March. Unofficial estimates cite three thousand Tibetan civilian deaths.

LHASA, 20th March. Machine gun fire killed over twenty Tibetan women inside the headquarters of the Women's Association.

LHASA, 20th March. Artillery fire has damaged the base of the Potala.

LHASA, 20th March. At night, the capital of Tibet looks like a ghost town. Everywhere there are signs of the army operations underway—signs of destruction and death. Stray dogs mutilate the corpses abandoned on the roads.

LONDON, 21st March. *The Daily Mail* published a long article on the Lhasa clashes. It cites 'reports from New Delhi.'

LHASA, 21st March. Lhasa Radio announced that 'the troops of the People's Liberation Army have been given the order to carry out punitive action against the clique of Tibetan traitors that has committed horrible crimes in the capital.' Lhasa radio also said that 'the Tibetan rebels have destroyed roads of vital importance for the national defence, blown up bridges and dams, brought down lampposts and telegraph poles and burnt buildings and offices of central government organisations.'

LHASA, 21st March. A new, massive attack on the Norbulingka by Chinese artillery. There have been more Tibetan civilian victims.

LHASA, 21st March. The medical college, transformed into a military stronghold by Tibetan army soldiers, has capitulated. For almost ten hours the Chinese subjected it to massive bombarding. All the Tibetan soldiers and volunteers defending it have been killed.

LHASA, 21st March. Tibetan spies report that the Chinese are preparing the final assault on the Jokhang. The Central Cathedral is full to bursting with Tibetan refugees.

LHASA, 22nd March. The first mortar shell hit the Jokhang's golden roof at dawn. The Chinese attack on the last rampart of the Tibetan resistance has begun.

LHASA, 22nd March. Chinese soldiers are pushing their way with bursts of machine gun fire through the crowds that have rushed in to save the Jokhang. Three Chinese tanks have appeared in the streets adjoining the Central Cathedral.

LHASA, 22nd March. The battle in front of the Central Cathedral has been raging for three hours. The entire area has been transformed into a battle camp. Despite their huge losses, the Tibetans are resisting. A Chinese tank has been set fire to. Women are throwing stones and burning bottles from the rooftops of their homes at People's Liberation Army soldiers.

LHASA, 22nd March. The Chinese tanks, backed by armoured vehicles, have destroyed the barricades erected by the people of Lhasa. Two tanks now stand in front of the entrance to the Jokhang.

LHASA, 22nd March. At two in the afternoon, the loudspeakers at the street corners began to transmit announcements by General Tan Guansan and Minister Ngabo. General Tan Guansan ordered the citizens of Lhasa to 'lay down arms.' 'Those who do so will be pardoned;' the general said. Then it was Ngabo's turn. The Tibetan minister said, 'This is Ngabo speaking to you and, as you know, I am a member of the kashag, the Tibetan government. All fighting must stop. This is an order from the Tibetan, not the Chinese government. The Tibetan government has in fact decided to put a stop to the revolt. The Dalai Lama has not been killed. He has been kidnapped against his will by a group of reactionaries. Go back to your work. Lay down your arms and you will remain free.'

CHENYE (TIBET), 22nd March. The Dalai Lama's march through the south of his country continues. The group accompanying the Tibetan 'God-King' is now one hundred strong. It is escorted by three hundred and fifty Tibetan army soldiers and fifty Khampa warriors on horseback. During the day the fugitives separate into small groups so as not to be spotted by Chinese aircraft overflying the area.

LHASA, 22nd March. Lhasa Radio announced that 'over four thousand Tibetan rebels have been taken prisoner. Eight thousand weapons of different makes, eighty light and heavy machine guns, twenty-seven 81-mm mortar guns, six mountain cannon and ten million rounds of ammunition have been confiscated from the rebels.'

LHASA, 23rd March. The flag of the People's Republic of China with its five stars flutters over the Potala, the most symbolic building in Tibet. Lhasa Radio broadcast the news with the following words: 'Moved by a light breeze, the Chinese national flag, symbol of light and happiness, flutters over Lhasa. The red flag hereby greets the renaissance of this ancient city.'

LHUNTSE DZONG (TIBET), 27th March. The Dalai Lama and his followers reached Lhuntse Dzong, a small town with an old fort in southern Tibet. Over one thousand Tibetans made way for the procession of Tibet's 'God-King', burning incense and throwing votive scarves as he passed. At the entry to the fort the monks greeted him with sacred music.

In the late morning today an official in the Dalai Lama's retinue read a proclamation announcing the formation of a provisional Tibetan government. Tenzin Gyatso, fourteenth Dalai Lama of Tibet, has signed the proclamation, a copy of which has been sent to all the major towns in the country.

BEIJING, 28th March. The Chinese Prime Minister Zhou Enlai has signed a Cabinet order dissolving the Tibetan government. Its functions will be carried out by the Preparatory Committee of the

Autonomous Region of Tibet (PCART). Ngabo Ngawang Jigme has been nominated Vice-President of PCART. Eighteen PCART members, all part of the retinue of the Dalai Lama and all of whom have fled Lhasa with him, have been singled out as 'leaders of the rebellion.' Among them are the protocol chief Phala and Tibetan government minister Surkhang. The Cabinet order states that the rebels will be 'severely punished.' If they are captured, they all risk the death penalty.

KARPO-LA PASS (SOUTHERN TIBET), 28th March. A Chinese transport aircraft spotted the Dalai Lama and his retinue just after they crossed the pass. The band of fugitives immediately separated into several small groups. A sudden sandstorm reduced visibility considerably, preventing new sightings by Chinese aircraft.

CHU DHANGMO (INDO-TIBETAN BORDER), 31st March. Visibly ill, the Dalai Lama reached the border between Tibet and India on the back of a dzo (a cross between a cow and a yak). Six Gurkha soldiers standing to attention under a bamboo arch welcomed Tenzin Gyatso onto Indian territory. Their commanding officer offered the Dalai Lama a 'khata', the ceremonial white silk scarf.

TAWANG (INDIA), 3rd April. An Indian government official consigned a telegram signed Jawaharlal Nehru, Prime Minister of the Indian Union, to the Dalai Lama. The telegram read, 'My colleagues and I personally offer you our welcome and our sincerest congratulations on having arrived in India safe and sound. We are pleased to offer you, your family and your retinue all the assistance required for your stay in this country.'

TEZPUR (INDIA), 7th April. The people of Tezpur joyfully received the Dalai Lama on his arrival in this North-East Frontier Agency (NEFA) town. The temporal and spiritual head of Tibet received thousands of telegrams welcoming him to India. Awaiting the Dalai Lama were over one hundred journalists and photographers sent by all the major world news organisations to cover 'the event of the year.'

10th March 1999.
Forty years later.
In McLeod Ganj the sky was overcast. It was cold and it looked as if it might snow.

At a quarter past eight in the morning we were all in front of the Tsuglagkhang building. There were coloured banners everywhere — green, yellow, pink, white, red and blue. The writing on them was in Tibetan, Hindi and English.

One banner read:

ON THE 40TH ANNIVERSARY OF TIBETAN NATIONAL
UPRISING DAY
WE PAY TRIBUTE TO OUR BRETHREN WHO HAVE
SACRIFICED THEIR LIVES FOR TIBET'S FREEDOM.

On another banner was written:

STOP SENDING CHINESE SETTLERS TO TIBET.
TIBETANS ARE BECOMING
A MINORITY IN THEIR OWN COUNTRY.

There was a quotation from the Dalai Lama:

OUR WAY MAY BE LONG AND DIFFICULT
BUT I BELIEVE THAT TRUTH
WILL ULTIMATELY TRIUMPH.

Sitting on the ground in the centre of the square were the students of the Tibetan Children's Village (TCV). On the sides stood the Tibetan population of McLeod Ganj, Dharamsala and the neighbouring towns. Young and old alike had green ribbons around their foreheads with the words 'FREE TIBET', 'TIBET 1959-1999' or 'SAVE TIBET'.

At eight-thirty the TCV band arrived. The flutes and drums covered the sound of the other instruments. The young musicians were wearing pea-green short-sleeved shirts and blue trousers. The standard bearer preceded them, strutting along stiffly. He wore a fur cap on his head. The flag he carried was that of independent Tibet.

At nine o' clock on the dot the Dalai Lama arrived, walking at a hurried pace. Four elderly monks accompanied him. Tenzin Gyatso went to seat himself on the small wooden throne placed in the centre of the Main Temple veranda.

Seated around the sides of the veranda were the members of Parliament, dignitaries and illustrious guests. Among them, in the last few rows, was the American actor Richard Gere.

The 'kalon' (minister) Sonam Topgyal raised the flag. The colours of independent Tibet swirled in the grey sky heavy with rain clouds. At the centre of the flag were two snow lions, coloured white and green. They carried the symbols of the 'three jewels' — the Buddha, the Dharma and the Sangha. In the background were the twelve red and blue rays of a golden sun rising from behind a snow-covered mountain. The band played the national hymn. The students of the Tibetan school sang along lustily.

The last verse said: 'That the spread of the Buddha's teachings in the ten directions/bring happiness and peace;/ That the life and the wisdom of Tibet prevail / In the fight against dark, negative forces.'

Sonam Topgyal requested a minute of silence 'to pay homage to the one million two hundred thousand martyrs who sacrificed their lives to free Tibet.' The standard bearer laid down his flagpole.

The Dalai Lama lowered his eyes, an expression of sorrow on his face.

The official speeches followed, all in Tibetan. Two ministers of the government in exile spoke first. During their long speeches Topden, a friend of mine, handed me two typewritten pages. 'Read it,' he said in a low voice. It was an English translation of an anonymous letter from Lhasa.

The letter read: 'Tenth March — today is the day when the Tibetan people lost their beloved homeland. On this day they also lost tranquillity of mind and the relative harmony of their traditional lifestyle. But, what is more, they lost their legitimate right to remain a free and independent nation. Today is the day when the United Nations and the international community shamelessly allowed the monster of the twentieth century, Red China, to massacre the tiny, peace-loving people of Tibet.

'After living under Chinese occupation for forty years the Tibetan people, especially the younger generation, firmly maintain their belief that Tibet is a separate nation from China. Tibet and China are two entirely different countries geographically, culturally, historically and spiritually. The so-called Tibetans who have benefited from the Chinese occupation do not represent the majority of Tibetan people. The majority, the farmers and nomads, are still living in tumbledown mud houses and following the tracks of their yaks. They possess nothing. What they possess is the memory of the Dalai Lama, their religious culture and their traditional Tibetan way of life.

'In the depths of our hearts we despair. But we remain aware and in control of our minds because we believe there is justice which, although it still seems far away from the Roof of the World, will one day appear in Tibet.'

After the two ministers of the government in exile had spoken, it was the Dalai Lama's turn. He read his speech in a firm baritone.

'My sincere greetings to my compatriots in Tibet and in exile, and to all our friends and supporters all over the world, on the occasion of the fortieth anniversary of the Tibetan national uprising of 1959.

'Four decades have passed since we went into exile. We

have continued our struggle for freedom within and outside Tibet. Four decades are a considerable time in a person's life. Many fellow countrymen, those who stayed in Tibet in 1959 and those who left, are gone. Today, second and third generation Tibetans shoulder the responsibility of our freedom struggle. They do so with undiminished determination and indomitable spirit.

'During our four decades of life in exile, the Tibetan community has gone through increasing democratisation. We have made tremendous progress in education. We have also preserved our unique cultural and religious heritage. Our achievements on these fronts are widely recognised by the international community.

'During the same four decades, Tibet has been under the complete control of the government of the People's Republic of China. The Chinese authorities have had a free hand in governing our country. The late Panchen Lama's *70,000-Character Petition* of 1962 is a telling historical document on draconian Chinese actions in Tibet. The immense destruction and human suffering during the Cultural Revolution are known worldwide. In January 1989, a few days before his death, the Panchen Lama stated that the progress of Tibet under China could not match the destruction and suffering inflicted on the Tibetan people. Despite some development and economic progress, Tibet faces many fundamental problems.

'The root cause of the Tibetan problem is not a different ideology and social system or the clash between tradition and modernity. Nor is it the issue of human rights violations alone. The root of the Tibetan issue lies in Tibet's long, separate history, its distinct and ancient culture and its unique identity.

'The plight of the Tibetan people and our non-violent freedom struggle have touched the hearts and consciences of all those who cherish truth and justice. Today, the Tibetan freedom movement is in a much stronger position than before. I firmly believe that despite the present intransigence of the Chinese government, there are good prospects for meaningful dialogue and negotiation today. I appeal to governments, parliaments and our friends to continue their support with renewed vigour. I believe such expressions of international support are essential. They are vital in communicating to Beijing the need to seriously address the Tibet issue.

'Today, the tenth of March, I pay homage to the brave men and women of Tibet who died for the cause of our freedom. I pray for an early end to the suffering of our people.'

At the end of the ceremony the Dalai Lama shook hands with the band members and the school children. Then, once again moving quickly, he crossed the path that led to his private quarters.

The entire audience was on its feet.

Meanwhile, the head of the procession was forming on the other side of Tusglagkhang. It would cover the three kilometres of the short cut from McLeod Ganj to Dharamsala.

The leading banner read: 'WE SUPPORT AND STAND FOR THE CAUSE OF TIBET'. It was signed 'Taxi union'.

Tens of flags of independent Tibet followed.

Tibetans of all ages took part in the procession. There were children from the Tibetan Children's Village in their white and blue checked shirts. There were girls from the high school in green chubas and grey pullovers. There were youngsters from the Tibetan Youth Congress in denim jeans and Di Caprio haircuts. There were old ladies with tangled hair, in black clothing covered by aprons with thin coloured stripes.

The most combative section of the procession was the monks'. Their robes were spattered with mud. They made fists and shouted slogans.

Seen from afar, the monks' section looked like a giant earthworm slowly making its way along the hill.

All the Tibetan shops in McLeod Ganj and Dharamsala had their shutters down. The schools were closed.

At half past midday the procession reached the District Courts, the demonstration's arrival point.

There were more speeches. More slogans were shouted through the loudspeakers.

A short way away, in a small grassy clearing, Tibetan Youth Congress militants set fire to a life-size cloth dummy. It wore blue overalls with a red collar. It had a 'Made in China' Thermos flask tied to its side and the flag with five stars of the People's Republic of China. At the puppet's feet was a small stack of Chinese goods—Thermoses, fans and towels. As the flames licked at each object, people applauded.

As the demonstration proceeded, I jotted down all the slogans.

A lone voice shouted the first part and the entire procession chorused the second.

'Gyamar Bod ne—Thardol chig.' 'Chinese—Out of Tibet.'

'What do we want? We want justice.'

'Tibet belongs to? Tibetans.'

'Yahi hamara nara hai—Tibbat desh hamara hai.' 'This is our cry — Tibet is our country.'

'Dilo jaan se pyaara—Desh hamara.' 'We love our country more than our lives.'

'San unees so basat—Yaad karo.' 'Don't forget 1962' (the year the Indo-Chinese war took place).

'Tibbat mein athyachar—Band karo.' 'Stop the atrocities in Tibet.'

'Jaan bhi dhenge, khoon bhi dhenge—Desh ke mitti na dhenge.' 'We'll give our lives and our blood, but we won't give up our land.'

'Save Tibet.'

'What do we want?' 'We want freedom.'
'Long live Dalai Lama.'
'U.N.O. — We want justice.'
'Stop genocide in Tibet.'
'Tibbat ki azaadi—Bharat ki suraksha.' 'Tibetan independence is the safety of India.'
'Release Panchen Lama.'
'Red Chinese—Go back.'
'Wake up, wake up—U.N.O.'
'Zindabad, zindabad—Dalai Lama zindabad.' 'Long life, long life — long life to the Dalai Lama.'
'Murdabad, murdabad—Jiang Zemin murdabad.' 'Down with, down with—down with Jiang Zemin.'
'Param puja Dalai Lama ki jai.' 'Long live His Holiness the Dalai Lama.'
'Bod rangzen—Tsangma yin.' 'Tibet is independent.'
'Stop killing in Tibet.'
'Chini—Hindi bhai-bhai—Yahi Chin ka dhoka hai.' 'The Chinese and Indians are brothers—That's China's lie.'
'Choro choro, Tibbat choro—Bhago bhago, Chinya bhago.' 'Leave, leave, leave Tibet—run, run, run home Chinese.'
'Down with China.'
'Bod kyi dagpo—Bod mi yin.' 'Tibet belongs—to the Tibetans.'
'U.N.O.—Keep your promise.'
'You are the butcher—China.'
'Tibet for? — Tibetans.'
'Bharat Tibbat metri—Amar rahe.' 'Long live Indo-Tibetan friendship.'
'Long live Panchen Lama.'
'Dalai Lama—Zindabad.' 'Long live the Dalai Lama.'
'Jiang Zemin—Murdabad.' 'Down with Jiang Zemin.'
'Tibbat desh — Hamara hai.' 'Tibet is our country.'
'Chin ka Tibbat pe athyachar—Bharat ke liye kahtra hai.' 'Chinese atrocities in Tibet are a danger for India.'

'Jaan se bhi pyaara—Desh hamara.' 'We love our country more than life itself.'

'Jab tak suraj chand rahega—Tibet desh hamara rahega.' 'As long as the sun and moon shine, Tibet will be our land.'

Refugees

I began to visit the refugee camp of Majnu ka Tilla in 1972. That year I had enrolled in a course in modern Chinese at Delhi University.

To get to the university, I had to take a bus that went through all of Old Delhi.

In those days the buses weren't numbered. The conductor would stand on the rear step and call out the remaining stops along the route.

At the I.T.O. stop the buses merely slowed down. You had to jump into a moving bus.

The old town began after Delhi Gate.

Dariya Ganj was always teeming. The facades of the buildings, darkened by the monsoon, were covered with advertisements: 'GWALIOR SUITING', 'DELCO SHOES', 'SONYO CAR RADIOS'.

There were old Indian Communist Party (Marxist) posters on a wall with peeling plaster:

> KISSINGER OF DEATH
> GO BACK.
> NIXON-YAHYA
> CO-PARTNERS IN CRIMES
> AGAINST BANGLADESH.

Beyond Darya Ganj the cityscape extended to include the two most important monuments in Old Delhi. To the right was the superb Red Fort. To the left was the Jama Masjid mosque.

The Chandni Chowk crossroads was one of the most congested points in India. Thousands of pedestrians. Bicycles.

Pedal rickshaws. Farm carts with rubber tyres drawn by emaciated zebus. Dromedaries. Elephants.

Once you got to Ajmeri Gate you left behind the din of the old town.

The university students would be the only ones left on the bus.

We would cross the Civil Lines area with its low houses hidden behind banyan trees.

Finally, on Mall Road, we would come to a stop in front of the university campus.

I enrolled in my Chinese course in August 1972, a few weeks after the American President Richard Nixon's 'historic' visit to the People's Republic of China.

Relations between China and the West would be normalised and one day, I thought, I too would be able to visit Beijing.

The Chinese professor was called Tan Chung. His classes were wonderful. Tan Chung would tell us the original meaning of Chinese characters.

'In Mandarin you say "bu" for "no",' he would explain. 'The character is made up of four strokes. There is one horizontal stroke on top and, below, another three signs that form the tip of an arrow. The horizontal stroke represents the sky. The "tip of the arrow" is actually a bird with open wings.' Then Professor Tan Chung would add, 'If you have a bird and you keep it prisoner in your fist and then release it to fly towards the sky, will the bird come back to you? "No".'

I worked hard studying Chinese because I hoped to be able to go to Beijing on a scholarship.

But my real dream was different. I wanted to get to Lhasa, Tibet.

I said as much to Raj, one of my classmates.

'If that's what you want,' Raj told me, 'Tibet is here, a stone's throw away.'

He told me there was a Tibetan refugee camp not far from Delhi University. The camp was called Majnu ka Tilla. One day Raj took me there on his sputtering old Enfield. There were about fifty wooden hovels in the refugee camp, all covered with stitched-up army tent scraps. The huts were crushed together on a sandy expanse between Mall Road and the Yamuna river.

Swollen by the monsoon, the river ran luminously between ranks of low vegetation and heaps of garbage.

The Tibetans of Majnu ka Tilla made a living selling 'chang,' beer made of fermented barley. A plate of noodles and two mugs of chang cost two rupees and seventy-five paise. Many of the university students ate lunch at the Majnu ka Tilla dhabas.

As the years passed, I watched the refugee camp get bigger. By 1979 it had become a real village. Over two thousand people lived there.

Open sewers ran all the way round the wooden hovels. There was a little temple too. Inside it was an enormous prayer barrel covered in thin copper foil. On the altar stood a black and white photograph of the Dalai Lama. He was young and wore glasses with a heavy black plastic frame. He looked like a good university student.

For years, I collected the stories of the Tibetan refugees at Majnu ka Tilla. Many of their tales were written in blood[1].

SONAM NYIMA was 42 years old. He was a well-built fellow with strong, muscular arms. He had a chang belly pressing against his vest.

He carried his two-year-old daughter in his arms. The little

---

1. To protect the identity of the people interviewed, their names have been changed and their places of birth omitted.

girl was wearing a dress with red and blue embroidery on it. She had two tiny plastic bracelets on her wrists and her eyes were ringed with lampblack.

'I ran away from Tibet with my wife Dawa. We had only been married a short time. Life in Tibet had become impossible. The members of my family had been classified "average peasants." They were constantly being accused of crimes they hadn't committed. I decided to escape. The Chinese came to know about it. They accused me of "abandoning the master path of the proletarian socialist revolution to join the reactionary bandits of the Dalai.' At my re-education sessions they told me: "Those who run away to imperialist countries instead of working for the Motherland are making a serious mistake. Those who have gone into exile are now suffering the torments of hell. Many of them have died of hunger or because of the great heat. Only a handful of reactionaries are left with the Dalai now."

'The Chinese say that there is religious freedom in Tibet. That's not true. You can't recite the "Om mani padme hum" mantra. Anyone who prays is considered a "reactionary" and is continually accused of remaining attached to "superstitious practices."

'During the Cultural Revolution, the Red Guards forced us to destroy the monasteries in our country. The wooden blocks with which books were printed were used as firewood. The terracotta statues were thrown out into the roads and smashed to smithereens. The books were set on fire. Everything of value was taken to China.

'We had to learn quotations from Mao's *Red Book* by heart. There were patrols of Red Guards on the roads. They were called "Safety Groups". They would stop people and ask them to recite passages from the *Red Book*. Anyone who wasn't able to would be severely punished.

'The Chinese exploited the Tibetans' labour and took away most of our farm produce. In fact, we have become the slaves of a foreign power. They are always telling us about a "third world war". The entire population between fifteen and sixty years of age is kept under constant pressure.

'It took us nine days to escape from Tibet. We walked mostly at night.

'A few months after we arrived in India my wife got sick. She died very quickly.

'Some years ago I remarried. Now I get by selling chang here in Majnu ka Tilla.

'I spend all the little money I earn on repairs to the tent that covers my hut. During the monsoon the wind and the rain keep destroying it.'

LOBSANG DHUNDUP was 54 years old, with protruding ears and a look of sadness in his eyes. Deep lines furrowed his brow. He had a moustache clipped short bordering his upper lip. His lanky frame was dressed in only a vest and a pair of khaki shorts. He was barefoot. He had a dense network of prominent veins on his feet and the backs of his hands.

'I was a soldier in the Tibetan army. In 1959, after the popular uprising in Lhasa, I joined the anti-Chinese guerrillas. I ended up in prison. During the day they made us work on a power station construction site. We had to carry heavy loads on our backs. Many prisoners died of exhaustion. Later I was transferred to Drapchi prison, where food rations were practically non-existent. They gave us hot water twice a day and broth with a few beans and peas once, at lunch. Since we didn't have either plates or bowls, they made us eat in the same containers in which we urinated at night.

'Hundreds of prisoners died. When we entered the prison they would take away our shoelaces and belts so we wouldn't use them to commit suicide.

'We were continually subjected to interrogations. They wanted to know everything about the guerrillas—who the bosses were, where they worked, what their plans were.

'I was subjected to continuous torture. They would ask me to confess my "crimes." They would tell me it was useless to remain silent, since they already had a vast amount of information about me.

'After three years of this life the Chinese let me out of prison. They had probably understood that I was not in a position to give them any important information.

'In Tibet, the Tibetans have a very hard life. The "state tax on grain" pushes people into starvation.

'The Chinese propaganda keeps talking about a forthcoming revolutionary war that will involve the whole world.

'Everyone gets mobilised in war preparations—men and women, the young and the old.

'Despite the Chinese repression the Tibetans continue to have faith in the Dalai Lama. They still hope that one day he can come back to a free and happy Tibet.'

DAWA DORJEE was 36. He was a thickset man with a short neck and a flat nose like a boxer's. He had watery eyes that always seemed on the verge of tears. He was bare-chested and had a white shirt twisted round his head to protect him from the sun.

'I spent four years and six months in prison in Tibet. During my prison term they transferred us to the foothills of a mountain for a few months to cut trees and make boards out of them. Three prisoners tried to escape. Their leader was executed before our eyes, with a bullet through the back of his head. The other two were tortured for days on end. They died too.

'Another two prisoners committed suicide by throwing themselves into a river. Many died of hunger and privation.

'When I was released they told me not to talk about my prison experience. "Otherwise we'll kill you," they said.

'Today, it's practically impossible to travel inside Tibet. You have to ask the Chinese for permission to do anything. Groups of more than three people can't eat together in public places.

'We have had to abandon all our traditional values. "The reactionaries will never go away by themselves," the Communist Party officials would tell us. "It is the people who have to destroy them."

'They forced us to raze our village monastery to the ground. Everything of value was carried to China. The pages of our Buddhist texts were set on fire or used as toilet paper.

'People were forced to learn quotations from Mao Zedong by heart. The Chinese would tell us that the *Red Book* contained all of Mao's revolutionary ideas. These ideas had to "inspire our everyday life."

'Ever since the people's communes were set up, everything in Tibet has been collectivised—cultivable land, animals, agricultural implements. Almost all of the commune's produce is taken away by the Chinese, who call it "patriotic grain tax". There is always scarcity. People die of hunger. Many commit suicide by hanging themselves or throwing themselves into rivers in flood.

'In my village they launched a "campaign for class cleansing". In the course of long public sittings everyone above eight years of age would be forced to confess their "crimes." They would have to declare whether they opposed Chinese policies in Tibet. Whether they had criticised the Communist

Party. Whether they had ever thought of rebelling. Whether they still hoped for Tibetan independence. The confessions were extorted through blows and torture. Many people ended up in prison. Others were executed.

'In Tibet, the Chinese deny the Tibetans any form of liberty. No one can pray any more. Private property has been abolished. Parents no longer have the right to decide the future of their children. Children are taken away from their families and the Chinese teach them whatever they want to. The Chinese propaganda is revolting. They call the Dalai Lama "a butcher with bloody hands who fed off the flesh of his people".'

PHURBU TSERING was 54 years old. He was a short, plump man. He wore a Hawaiian shirt and a pair of shorts that left his muscular legs bare. His hair and moustache were black and so were the frames of his spectacles. Under the thick lenses was a pair of small, bright eyes. He spoke excitedly, gesticulating all the while.

'Life in Lhasa is very precarious. A worker with a strong constitution would earn eighteen kilos of unrefined tsampa[2] and four hundred and fifty grams of butter every month. A weak worker would earn half that. All the Tibetan shops in Lhasa were shut down. The few available goods could only be bought in Chinese shops. Many people died of hunger. Two or three carts heaped with dead bodies would come out of Drapchi prison every day. Often, these corpses were used to fertilise the soil. No one was allowed to say openly that people were dying because food was scarce.

'No Tibetan could enter the Potala. The Jokhang was only open to the public in the morning. We could go to visit it briefly, but not to pray. At night, there was no yak's butter lamp burning in the shrine.

2. Roasted barley wheat

'The Chinese used the libraries of the three big monasteries in the suburbs of Lhasa as warehouses. All the sacred images in gold and silver were taken to China. The iron, copper and bronze items were melted down to make weapons and ammunition. The pages of our sacred books were used to wrap merchandise in the Chinese shops.

Before the Chinese came there were over 18,000 monks at Ganden, Drepung and Sera. Today there are fifty at most in each of these three monasteries.

'They forced the monks and nuns to have sex in public in front of the Jokhang.

'The Tibetans no longer have the right to live in their homes. The Chinese shift people around as they please. Since the houses don't belong to anyone anymore, no one repairs them. This way the old buildings in Lhasa are going to ruin. The Chinese have built their own houses in Lhasa's most beautiful parks.

'It is very difficult to get out of Lhasa. You have to ask the Chinese authorities for permission. You have to declare where you want to go and who you want to meet.

'The Tibetans are forced to work like animals. They no longer have any freedom. The entire city of Lhasa has been transformed into one big prison.'

PASSANG was 67. He was lying on a length of sackcloth along the river's edge. He was practically naked. He had only a strip of white cloth wrapped around his bony hips. He had a face full of wrinkles, a big hooked nose, a grey moustache and sparse white down along his chin. He was toothless and had a perennial smile stamped on his mouth.

'The Chinese came to our village and told us, "China and India have links that go back a long way. That is why the Indian government has decided to send back all the reactionaries who have abandoned Tibet. So running away is useless. Even if you manage to do it, you will immediately be sent back and severely punished. These are the rules established by the Communist government of this country. The same rules also say that you must hand over all the weapons and ammunition in your possession."

'The assembly hall of the monastery near our village began to be used for political trials. The rest of the monastery was used as stables and warehouses. One day some low-flying aeroplanes passed. They threw out leaflets. It was written on them that there are only two paths, the one that leads to the Motherland and the wrong one that leads to the reactionary 'Dalai'. "People have to lay down their arms and give themselves up. Those who decide to follow the reactionary 'Dalai' or run away to America will be annihilated."

'When they started their land reform, I was put in the 'poor peasant' category. We had to work from nine in the morning to six in the evening in the communes. Then, every night, there were three hours of 'study sessions'. They would tell us about the great successes China had obtained as a result of President Mao's brilliant leadership. Whereas we were literally dying of hunger.

'I managed to escape on my third try.'

GYALTSEN DILMA was a 39-year-old woman. Her hair was tied in a braid on the nape of her neck. She had a high forehead and an open, likeable face. She wore a crumpled grey chuba. The blouse was made of printed cotton. She had a necklace of uneven stones threaded on a string. Her teeth were uneven too. She showed them the few times she broke into a half-smile.

'There had been a bad harvest in China for many years. Large quantities of grain, barley, peas and butter were transported by air from Tibet to the "Motherland". In my town, after the harvest, long convoys of army trucks carried away quintals and quintals of barley. People protested. The Chinese would tell us that that the barley was being given to Tibetan nomads in the north of the country. They would say to us: "Recently, some reactionaries have been circulating malicious rumours to the effect that we are transporting barley to China. The Chinese don't eat tsampa. So what would we do with all your barley?" But we all knew that the nomads came to buy their barley in the towns.

'When the people's communes were set up, many, many people died of hunger. There were dead bodies everywhere. Everyone from eight to seventy-five years old had to work in the communes. Those who worked would be given a spoonful of tsampa per day. The old people and children didn't get anything. Their families had to help them.

'People were forced to eat weeds or live on carrion in order to survive. The Chinese propaganda kept on saying that the "third world war" was about to break out. We had to increase production and save as much as possible. The result was that the Tibetans had nothing to eat any more and no clothes to wear. Most of the commune's produce ended up in the "state grain reserve" and the "war preparation reserve." There were revolutionary committees everywhere. The Chinese propaganda was suffocating. The children were taught some Tibetan in the early years of school. Then nothing. As a result, most young Tibetans now only speak Chinese.

'The young were taught to deride their culture and their religion. Instead they had to sing the praises of Mao Zedong and the Chinese Communist Party. Traditional Tibetan clothing was forbidden. Men and women all wore blue jackets and baggy trousers. There are Chinese soldiers everywhere in Tibet. The number of suicides among Tibetans keeps increasing.'

JIGME NAMGYAL was 61 years old. His head was fully shaven. His eyes were two narrow slits in a sunburned leather mask. He carried a rosary with ivory beads in his left hand. With his right hand he turned a prayer wheel.

'When the Chinese invaded our land we told them that ours was an independent country, separate from China. We had lived our way for thousands of years and we had no need of their help and much less of 'reforms' instituted by foreigners. In reply the Chinese would tell us that soon they would conquer the whole world and that our desire for independence was ridiculous. Many Tibetans finished in prison. They were beaten black and blue in jail. The Chinese arrested many monks and lamas. They made them drink urine and eat human excrement. The monasteries were plundered and demolished. Anyone who was caught praying was arrested.

'For over a year, for two hours each evening, they forced us to study five books titled *The Stages of Socialism*. They would teach us the "four big oppositions-opposition to religion, opposition to personal power, opposition to privileges, opposition to counter-revolutionaries."

'The entire population of our country was divided into five work groups. The old and the sick were given the task of taking the animals out to pasture. Nine and ten-year-old children were divided into teams. Each had the job of hunting birds. Every evening, they had to show the Chinese their catch. The group with the smallest number of dead birds was severely punished.'

CHOEKYI UAMO was 29 years old. She had prominent cheekbones and thick lips. Her straight black hair was loose and fell down her back. She wore a short pea-green blouse that she hitched up every so often to breastfeed her baby.

'I ran away from Tibet with my parents when I was little

more than a child. My father and mother are dead now. It was hard for them to die in a foreign country. I don't remember much about Tibet. But my parents would often talk to me about it. They told me that when the Chinese arrived, everything changed. My father would say that the entire country had been turned into a prison.

'During the Cultural Revolution, the attack on our religion reached its climax. All the religious buildings were razed to the ground. Tibetan Communist Party cadres destroyed them. The Chinese limited themselves to giving orders.

'My mother used to tell me that men and women were forbidden to wear traditional Tibetan clothing. People had to cut their hair short. Rings, necklaces and earrings were banned. Everyone had to memorise quotations from Mao's *Red Book*. In those days many people gave up all hope. They thought our whole country would be destroyed. Many Tibetans committed suicide. They hung themselves, stabbed themselves in the heart or threw themselves into rivers. My parents decided to run away. We reached the Nepal border after eight nights of forced march.

'Here in Delhi I have found work in a small dispensary. That's why I can speak English now.'

***

In 1979 I received accreditation from the Indian government. I wrote my first article as India correspondent on the refugee camp of Majnu ka Tilla. I called it 'Does Tibet still exist?'

Lobsang Dolma

I interviewed Dr. Lobsang Dolma in August 1979. For the Tibetans it was the sixth month of the year 2016, the Year of the Earth Sheep. I had an appointment to see the doctor at her house in McLeod Ganj.

The white villa had been recently constructed. The clinic was on the ground floor and the doctor's residence on the first floor.

Lobsang Dolma had dressed up to the nines to be photographed. She wore a fire engine red blouse with floral motifs watermarked on it. Her chuba was beige and she had on a traditional Tibetan apron over it. Around her neck was a double string of 'zi' and coral with a heavy turquoise-studded pendant. It was the oldest and most precious of her family jewels.

I photographed the doctor on the terrace of her house. The parapet running around it hadn't been plastered yet.

Thousands of medicinal pills had been laid out in the sun to dry.

The doctor smiled at the camera lens, trying to hide slightly protruding teeth.

We returned to the first floor of the building. It was there that Lobsang Dolma told me the story of her life.

***

'The black clouds from the East
Will not obscure our sky forever.
One day the sun will chase the clouds away
And light our land up again.'

'I would sing this song in the evenings around the bonfire

of the refugee camp with the other Tibetan refugees. It was 1961. I had worked in India for almost a year on a construction site, building a road between Palampur and Lahaul in the Kullu valley.

'I spent ten hours a day breaking rocks and carrying stones on my back. Then I would walk for miles with my daughters, aged two and four, to return to the camp.

'It was in that period that, here in McLeod Ganj, I met the person who would change my life forever.

'But let me start at the beginning.

'I finished building this house a year ago. I've called it "Khangkar," "white house."

'Khangkar has had an important role in the history of my family.

'We should go back to the year 1042. It was then that the Indian sage Atisha was called to Tibet to preach Buddhism.

'After crossing Nepal, Atisha reached the Kyirong valley, the "land of happiness", in western Tibet. Here he was struck by the sight of a large mountain called "Pangkar". Atisha prophesied that the mountain would become famous one day. As time passed the name "Pangkar" changed to "Khangkar" or "white house."

'Two hundred years after the Indian sage's visit, there was a small white-painted hospital at the foot of the mountain.

'At the end of the fourteenth century the Khangkar hospital became one of Tibet's most important schools of medicine. The hospital gave free medical aid and medicines to anyone who needed them. My father, Doctor Tsering Wangdue, was the twelfth successive chief physician of Khangkar hospital.

'When my father became a widower he married his first wife's younger sister. I was born in 1935.

'Tibetan society had always been quite open to women. They enjoyed a certain amount of freedom and autonomy. But that wasn't the case in the arts and sciences. In these disciplines, the more conservative sections of society barred women entrance. My father was a courageous man. He decided that I would be the thirteenth chief physician of Khangkar hospital.

'I began studying medicine at fourteen. My teacher was Geshe Lungtok Nyima. At home, my father supervised my studies. There were over thirty students in my class. I was the only girl. I had good results. I was good at medicine and in philosophy and poem composition as well.

'Those were happy years. At harvest time the entire Kyirong valley took part in the "Shaschen," the "big dance," during which the local boys and girls competed in a contest of a hundred and four dances and songs. For years I was the leader of the girls' team.

'In 1950 I graduated in medicine. I started work with my father at the Khangkar hospital straightaway. Soon after I got married. My husband also started working at the hospital. He became an expert pharmacist.

'Life in Kyirong went on peacefully. The beauty of the landscape made life almost idyllic.

'But one day, out of the blue, everything changed. The Chinese arrived.

'They set up many military bases in our valley - one right next to our hospital.

'Every day the people were gathered to harvest. Everyone had to denounce his past. People started becoming suspicious. There were spies everywhere. No one talked anymore. The season of song and dance was over forever.

'My father, who formed part of the élite of the region, was arrested. They interrogated him. They asked him to renounce his religion. He refused. When he returned home, my father was near blind as a result of the torture he had been subjected to. He died a few weeks later.

'Shortly before he died, my father told me to run away from Tibet. He told me I would be able to continue being a doctor in exile. I would thereby be able to carry the lineage of the Khangkar hospital forward.

'One day I came to know that the Chinese wanted to send me to Beijing for a Marxist indoctrination course. There was no time to lose. I decided to escape.

'I left the hospital at night with my family. We walked for five nights and stayed hidden among the rocks during the day.

'At dawn on the sixth day we reached Nepal. It was the summer of 1959.

'In Nepal I continued my medical practice. In the summer I lived in Shapru, in the winter in Kathmandu.

'Then I decided to join the Tibetans who had followed the Dalai Lama into exile.

'In 1961 I arrived in Pathankot. The Indian government hired us as workers on construction sites, building the roads of the Kullu valley. It was back-breaking work, but I was happy. I had led my family to safety and I was free. And just as every Tibetan in Tibet wants to visit the sacred city of Lhasa at least once, so I wanted to visit Dharamsala, the Indian town that hosted the Dalai Lama.

'A group of women from my Kyirong district and I made a pilgrimage to the town in Himachal Pradesh. In Dharamsala we met lamas and dignitaries. We were given an audience and we prayed in the temple.

'Our last meeting was with Kyabje Trijiang Rinpoche, the Dalai Lama's second tutor. It was a meeting that changed my life.

'Trijiang Rinpoche asked me what I used to do in Tibet before coming to India in exile. He wanted to know where I had studied medicine. He tested my knowledge. He made me recite the texts I had learned by heart when I was young.

'In the end he told me it was important for me to start practising again.

'Trijiang Rinpoche suggested I apply to the Tibetan Medical College that had just been set up in McLeod Ganj.

'My application was refused.

'They told me there had never been a woman doctor in the entire history of the Mendzekhang. Instead, they sent me to the Dalhousie Tibetan School to look after pre-school children. There the principal of the school allowed me to open a small dispensary. Thus I began to practice as a doctor again.

'In 1972, the same Tibetan Medical College that had refused my application some years before offered me the post of chief physician. I accepted. I held the post until August 1978. For a year now I have had my own private clinic. I called it "Khangkar", "white house", after the clinic I had to abandon in Tibet after the arrival of the Chinese.

'Now my two daughters, Passang Gyalmo and Tsewang Dolkar, have also graduated in medicine here in McLeod Ganj. They will be the fourteenth generation of Khangkar hospital doctors.'

The doctor offered me Tibetan tea and biscuits. We moved down to the ground floor for the real interview. The lunch break was over and Lobsang Dolma had to start seeing her patients again.

There were many people, Indians as well as Tibetans, in the waiting room. They were all very poor. There was also the occasional young Western hippie, yellow from jaundice.

The doctor's room was very small. A large wooden table occupied most of it. Propped against the wall was a set of shelves with some voluminous dossiers on them. The files had 'epilepsy,' 'cancer,' 'leukaemia' and 'asthma' written on them. I sat down next to the doctor. Her first-born daughter, Pasang Gyalmo, assisted her. The first patient was an elderly Indian. Doctor

Lobsang Dolma placed the tips of the index, middle and ring fingers of her right hand on the pulse of the patient's left wrist. She half-closed her eyes to concentrate. She remained motionless for about two minutes.

The doctor then repeated the operation with the fingers of her left hand on the old Indian's right wrist. This time the test was rapid. 'You have diabetes,' the doctor said.

I asked Lobsang Dolma to unveil the mysteries of Tibetan medicine to me between one patient and the next.

'How did this medicine originate?' I asked.

She replied, 'Traditionally we trace our medicine back to the Buddha in his manifestation as the Buddha of Medicine. There is nothing astonishing about this. It was in fact the Buddha who cured all living beings of the suffering that derives from being part of "samsara". Historically it was in the seventh century, under the reign of Songsten Gampo, that the *Four Medical Tantras*, the essential texts of our medical literature, were compiled.'

'What are the causes of illness, according to Tibetan traditional medicine?'

'In Tibet we have a saying: "Ignorance is like a bird's shadow — it follows the bird even when it flies in the sky." This "basic ignorance" (*ma rig pa*) accompanies us from birth. And it is the remote cause of all our illnesses.

'Then there is a more immediate cause. Generally speaking, we can say that it is due to the lack of balance between the three fundamental humours of the human body - tripa, behken and lung. Tripa translates into "bile", behken as "phlegm" and lung as "wind." When the balance of bile, phlegm and wind is affected, these three humours become disease-causing agents.

'The disturbances that bile provokes are warm in nature

while those caused by phlegm are cool. Those derived from wind can be either warm or cool.

'There are five different types of each of these basic humours. So we have a total of fifteen sub-divisions of humours in the human body. Once their balance alters, the task of medicine is to try to re-establish it.'

'Help me to understand these three essential humours better.'

'Tripa, or bile, is associated with fire. It is light, oily, acrid and hot. Behken, or phlegm, is constituted of the water element. Its nature is sticky, fresh, heavy and delicate. Lung, or wind, is associated with air. Its nature is coarse, hard, cold, thin and mobile.

'The five types of bile act on digestion, eyesight and the skin. The five types of phlegm regulate the body's liquids and control its joints. The five types of wind act on respiration, muscular action and the gastro-intestinal, urinary and genital systems.

'Phlegm is the most important humour when we are young, bile when we are adults and wind when we grow old. As I said earlier, one small imbalance among these three humours can cause illness.'

'How do you diagnose an illness?'

'Tibetan doctors say, "Touch and look and you will know everything." The "touch" refers to the pulse analysis. The "look" refers to the urine test.

'Ninety-five per cent of all illnesses can be diagnosed precisely just by analysing the pulse. But it is not an easy technique to master. It requires years and years of study.

'First of all the doctor uses the fingers of his right hand to examine the pulse on the patient's left wrist. There is a symbolic value in this extending of the pulse to the doctor on the part of the patient. It contains an implicit request to transfer to him the strength he needs to get well.

'The three fingers with which the patient's pulse is examined are the index, the middle and the ring fingers. The three fingers must be aligned; they must neither touch each other nor be too widely spaced from each other. Two organs can be examined with each finger, the first with the upper part of the fingertip, the second with the lower part. The fingers touch the patient's pulse with different degrees of pressure. The pressure of the index finger is slight; it remains at skin level. The middle finger presses more markedly. It reaches the flesh. Finally, the pressure of the ring finger is strong enough to touch bone.

'More specifically, we examine the patient's heart with the upper part of the index finger of the right hand and the intestine with the lower part. With the upper part of the middle finger we test the spleen. With the lower part we test the stomach. Using the upper part of the ring finger we can understand the state of the left kidney. With the lower part we examine the uterus if the patient is a woman or the sperm canal in the case of a man.

'The exam is then repeated on the patient's right pulse, this time with the index, middle and ring fingers of the left hand.

'With the upper part of the index finger on the left hand we can test the working of the lungs. With the lower part, we check the large intestine. We use the upper part of the middle finger to examine the condition of the liver, the lower part that of the gall bladder. Finally, with the upper part of the ring finger of the left hand we can check the state of the right kidney and, with the lower part, that of the urinary bladder.

'The pulse test should be done in the morning, when the

sun is already high in the sky, but when it is not yet too hot. The day before the test, the patient should follow certain food and behaviour restrictions. He should avoid eating meat or drinking alcohol. He shouldn't strain himself physically or have sex and should sleep for seven or eight hours.

'The urine test also has specific rules. The evening before the test the patient should avoid drinking coffee, tea, beer or alcohol. He should also avoid cold foods.

'The patient should collect his urine on an empty stomach as soon as he wakes up. A first analysis should be done immediately, while the urine is still warm. It should then be re-analysed when it is tepid and finally when it is cold. The things the urine test takes into consideration are colour, smell, vapour, sediments and the bubbles that urine forms when it is shaken.

'While it is still warm, the urine of a healthy person is a light yellow colour. In our tradition we say that this urine is the colour of melted butter made with the milk of a "dri," a cross between a yak and a cow.

'In general we might say that the urine of a patient with an illness due to tripa (bile) will be reddish and dense, with an intense smell and a lot of vapour. The urine of a patient with an illness caused by behken (phlegm) will be clear, with very little odour or vapour but with a lot of froth. Finally, the urine of a patient with an illness due to lung (wind) will be watery and white-blue and will produce a lot of bubbles when shaken.'

'Once the illness has been identified, what is the cure?'

'The rebuilding of the balance among the three humours is obtained in four different ways - through the diet, through behaviour, through medicines and through external "therapies". These include baths, massages, bloodletting, moxibustion, acupuncture and surgery.

'Tibetan medical science rarely uses drastic techniques such as surgery. We prefer to handle illness with milder cures and respect for the body of the sick person.'

'What are the characteristics of Tibetan pharmaceuticals?'

'Unlike allopathic medicine which limits itself to attacking the illness by using chemical substances, Tibetan medicine is holistic and only uses natural substances, mostly herbs. Only a few medicines use precious metals and stones. These are divided into two categories — materials like gold and silver that can be melted, and those that cannot, such as turquoise, coral, lapis lazuli and pearls. Mercury also forms part of our pharmaceuticals. But before it is used it is treated at length to get rid of all its harmful effects.

'As I said, in the overwhelming majority of cases, herbs form the components of the medicinal pills.

'To cure sicknesses of a warm nature we would use medicines with cool characteristics and vice versa.

'The plants we use to cure 'warm' sicknesses must preferably grow in northern mountains, on slopes with a northern exposure. Those used for 'cold' illnesses must grow in southern valleys, on slopes with a southern exposure.

'The plants must be dried immediately after they are harvested. Medicinal plants of a cold nature are dried in the shade, in the open air. Those of a warm character are dried in the sun or close to a fire. The plants are then ground to powder and mixed. Certain medicines have up to twenty-five components.

'At this point the pills are made. We generally use very simple machinery. Then the pills are placed in a long cotton bag. Two men hold it at each end and shake the bag to make the pills inside roll up and down.

"This process goes on for a whole day. It removes air from inside the pills and prevents them being altered by bacteria over time.'

'What are the illnesses that Tibetan medicine cures most successfully?'

'Diabetes, arthritis, hepatitis and ulcers. I have personally also obtained good results in the treatment of cancer, especially breast cancer and leukaemia.'

'How does Tibetan medicine deal with cancer?'

'Our medicine which, as I mentioned earlier, considers illness an imbalance to be re-positioned, believes that cancer is a disease like any other. Our medical texts show fifty-four types of tumours. Each of these requires an appropriate medicine. These are generally 'precious pills.' But I should add that we Tibetans believe cancer to be a karmic illness and therefore also caused by actions in an earlier life. This is why we think that sometimes, besides medicines, it is also necessary to have the blessings of an important lama.'

Lobsang Dolma probably realised that I was perplexed. She instructed her daughter to bring her the dossier marked 'cancer' from the shelf on the wall. There were letters from cancer patients everywhere in the world whom Lobsang Dolma had cured.

We lingered over the case of Nadia, a Canadian woman. She had come to the little Khangkar hosiptal in McLeod Ganj when Western diagnoses gave her no hope of survival. 'Today we write to each other regularly,' Lobsang Dolma said with a smile.

The interview had already gone on for a few hours. I asked the doctor one last question.

'Tell me about death,' I said. 'Does the doctor have a specific role during a sick person's last few moments of life?'

'Once again it is the pulse that tells us if a patient is about to die. If the cause of imminent death is due to lung (wind), the pulse rate will be like a "fluttering flag." If the cause is tripa (bile) the pulse is like "the beating of the wings of a falcon that has sighted its prey." In this case the pulse trembles and beats intensely. In the case of an imminent death provoked by behken (phlegm), the pulse of the dying person will be like "saliva that drops to the ground from the mouth of a ruminating cow."

'We Tibetans believe that the moment preceding death is one of the most important in the existence of every human being. It is in that moment that the dying person determines the mental state in which he will enter the "bardo", the interval of time that follows death and precedes a new existence.

'In the moments before death, the dying person often loses the power of speech and his heart stops beating. This does not mean that he is dead. On the contrary, he is extremely, intimately sensitive and registers everything happening around him.

'In the West I have seen the bodies of the dead being moved taking them by the lower limbs. We believe that this is wrong. At the moment of death the doctor must lift the dying person's body slightly. It is at that moment, in fact, that the spirit seeks a way to leave the body. If the upper part of the dying person's body is touched, reincarnation can take place in one of the three superior spheres — those of the gods, the semi-gods and humans. By touching the lower part of the body one favours a reincarnation into the three lower spheres — those of animals, evil sprits and hell.

'Tibetan medicine once contained the practice of administering the patient a potion of herbs that would allow him to die quickly and painlessly. Then we realised that this practice was wrong. It hampered the dying person's entry into the bardo in full possession of his mind. Without the mind, the spirit of the dead person would find itself in great difficulty.

'Generally speaking, when the doctor understands from the pulse test that there is nothing to be done for the patient, he should stop administering him medicine. The sick person should be taken to a calm and silent place so that his death takes place peacefully[1].'

---

1. After having taken upon herself the suffering of thousands of sick people, Dr. Lobsang Dolma died suddenly on the evening of the 15th December 1989 in her house at McLeod Ganj. She was 55.

Gu-Chu-Sum

The brick-and-tin shops of the McLeod Ganj bazaar were located along two narrow, parallel roads, Temple Road and Jogibara Road.

Squeezed between the two roads was a small, brightly-coloured temple. Elderly Tibetans spun the prayer barrels in the little temple, creating a dull, whirring sound.

Along Jogibara Road, behind the 'Dr. Lobsang Dolma Khangkar Memorial Clinic,' was the fruit and vegetable market. Spinach, cauliflower, carrots and ginger were laid out on wooden boxes or spread on jute sacks on the road.

The season's fruit — apples, oranges and rotting bananas — was displayed on handcarts with bicycle wheels. The apples cost forty rupees a kilo.

An open sewer gurgled on the right side of the road. There was a smell of decaying vegetables.

Two cows swayed ahead among the people, dropping greenish dung on the road as they went.

There were the usual beggars ('Hello friend'). The road sloped downwards a little.

McLeod Ganj's 'Sub-Post Office' was situated on the raised ground floor of a dilapidated building. The first floor housed the 'Okay Café.'

There was a reception centre for Tibetan refugees, 'Dharamshala for Tibetan Refugees and Himalayan Buddhists. McLeod Ganj,' about twenty metres ahead, on the same side of the road.

It was a three-storey building with iron bars at the windows. On the ground floor was a 'General Store'. It sold candles, shampoo, toothpaste and incense sticks. There was a public washhouse that gave on to the road at one end of the building. The refugees were rinsing food off aluminium bowls. A photocopy was pasted on the wall. 'Dear Tibetans, there are a lot of dangerous and infectious sexually transmitted diseases in this world. NEVER FORGET THE RUBBER TUBE.'

The newly arrived refugees had sun-burned cheeks. They had pageboy haircuts with a fringe covering their foreheads. Their almond-shaped eyes watched the young Westerners meeting at the nearby 'Chocolate Log' restaurant curiously.

The smaller children played on the street. They made kung fu movements. They kicked their feet in the air, imitating the sound of a bullet shot with each kick.

In the winter, waves of refugees arrived in McLeod Ganj, taking advantage of reduced patrolling on the border by Chinese soldiers.

After the reception centre Jogibara Road curved sharply, with a steep drop into the valley on one side offering a beautiful view of the Dhaula Dhar mountain range. The highest peaks were streaked white with snow.

Then there was the 'Geden Choeling Nursery,' a convent of small, plump Tibetan nuns.

Another fifty metre or so and I glimpsed the curved facade of a red brick building among the pines. On the ground floor was the 'Lung-ta,' a Japanese restaurant.

A flag of independent Tibet was hung on the wall of the restaurant lobby. One of the pillars in the restaurant bore a small poster: 'This restaurant and all the furnishings of the Lung-ta building were donated by Shogo Hamada, the well-known Japanese rock and roll singer, thanks to the profits of the "Free Tibet" concert in Hiroshima on the 26th December 1999.'

The 'Today Special Set' at Lung-ta cost one hundred rupees. It was miso soup, vegetable croquettes, boiled rice and 'nasu okura no agebitashi' and a salad of cabbage and hardboiled eggs.

On the first floor of the Lung-ta building was the headquarters of the 'Go-Chu-Sum Movement of Tibet'.

I asked to speak to the president.

The 'venerable' Yeshe Togden was a thirty-three-year-old monk.

He was a stocky man with the hands of a peasant and a mild gaze. He came from Meldro Gungkar, a built-up town eighty kilometres east of Lhasa. He had twice participated in demonstrations to free Tibet. The Chinese had arrested him. He had been condemned to seven and a half months in prison. When he was released in 1991 he escaped to India. Now, like many others, he lived in exile in McLeod Ganj.

Yeshe Togden's small office had a green carpet and a brand new computer.

Yeshe Togden only spoke Tibetan. His secretary acted as interpreter.

'Gu-Chu-Sum is an organisation of Tibetan ex-political prisoners,' the president informed me. 'In Tibetan, gu, chu and sum are the numbers nine, ten and three. Nine stands for September, ten for October and three for March. Those were the months in which the three demonstrations marking the new cycle of the Tibetan struggle against Chinese oppression were organised. The three dates we wish to remember with the name of our organisation are the 27th September 1987, the 1st October of the same year and the 5th March 1988. There were other revolts in Tibet after the 1959 Lhasa insurrection. But the three demonstrations we refer to mark a new phase of our struggle. Now it is the younger generation that is protesting. They are the young Tibetans who were born and have grown up under the Communist Chinese regime. They are laymen and monks who did not know Tibet before the occupation.

Now these young people too are getting organised and taking to the streets to demonstrate against Chinese colonialism. They too demand independence.'

It was mainly from the accounts of the members of the Gu-Chu-Sum in McLeod Ganj that I was able to reconstruct what happened in Lhasa in September and October 1987 and in March the following year.

***

Gu: Nine (September 1987)
On Monday 21st September 1987 the Dalai Lama addressed the Human Rights Committee of the American Congress in Washington D.C.

He said, 'I propose that the whole of Tibet, including the eastern provinces of Kham and Amdo, be transformed into an "ahimsa" zone of peace and non-violence.'

On this occasion, the Dalai Lama presented his five-point peace plan for Tibet:
1. The transformation of the whole of Tibet into a zone of peace.
2. The abandonment of China's population transfer policy which threatens the very existence of the Tibetans as a people.
3. Respect for the Tibetan people's fundamental rights and democratic freedoms.
4. The restoration and protection of Tibet's natural environment and the abandonment of China's use of Tibet for the production of nuclear weapons and the dumping of nuclear waste.
5. The commencement of earnest negotiations on the future status of Tibet and relations between the Tibetan and Chinese peoples.

In his speech the Dalai Lama also said, 'The Tibetans and the Chinese are two distinct peoples, each with its own land, its own culture, its own language and lifestyle. The differences between various peoples should be recognised and respected.'

In Lhasa, the evening news on the television on the 25th September gave the Dalai Lama's visit to the United States sixty seconds of coverage. The commentary was harsh. The Dalai Lama was accused of wanting to 'divide the Motherland.'

In the days immediately following, the Communist Party of the Autonomous Region of Tibet decided to organise a series of demonstrations 'in support of the Chinese policy in Tibet and against the Dalai Lama and his secessionist activities.'

In Lhasa's Barkor, however, hand-written leaflets began appearing. They sang the praises of 'His Holiness the Dalai Lama'.

All through the week preceding the 27th September, hundreds of Tibetans visited the Drepung, Sera and Ganden monasteries. They made cash offerings to the monks and asked them to pray for the Dalai Lama.

The monks at Drepung discussed the situation at length. It was mainly the younger monks who met. They were all hardly older than twenty. Many of them said praying wasn't enough. Something concrete had to be done in support of the Dalai Lama.

They fixed a meeting on the morning of the 27th September in Lhasa, near the Barkor.

The night before, in the monastery, they fashioned the flag of independent Tibet from pieces of coloured cloth. Then they prayed in the chapel of Palden Lhamo, the deity who protects the Dalai Lama and all of Tibet.

In front of the image of Palden Lhamo they vowed that, if they were arrested, they would not betray their companions, even if their lives were at stake.

On the morning of the 27th September the young monks went into Lhasa a few at a time. They had a rendezvous at eight o' clock in a Barkor tea house.

In the tea house they decided to hold a demonstration in the circuit that runs all the way round the Jokhang, the Central Cathedral.

At nine, the monks came out of the tea house. There were twenty-one of them. They formed a little procession, with four monks holding open the Tibetan flag at the head.

All of them had their fists raised to the sky. They shouted slogans: 'Bod Rangzen' ('Free Tibet'), 'Kyabgon Dalai Lama khrilor tampar shog' ('May the Dalai Lama live for ten thousand years').

About a hundred people joined the demonstrators. They went around the Barkor circuit thrice. They then decided to demonstrate in front of the government headquarters of the Autonomous Region of Tibet. They went down Yuthog Lam, the large tree-lined avenue that started from the Barkor square. They found the way barred by Chinese policemen in anti-combat gear.

The policemen thrashed the twenty-one monks from the Drepung monastery till they drew blood. They were arrested, together with another four demonstrators.

In Lhasa the next day, a rumour spread that the twenty-one monks had been tortured. It was said that they had been hung from the ceiling by their wrists, and that poison had been injected into their veins. It was rumoured that they would be judged on the morning of the 6th October.

Tensions were running high in the Tibetan capital.

Chu: Ten (October 1987)

The 1st October, the anniversary of the birth of the People's Republic of China, was a national holiday in China.

On the same day, another protest demonstration against the Chinese occupation of Tibet had been organised in Lhasa's

Barkor.

This time it was the monks from the Sera monastery who were demonstrating. There were twenty-three monks, all twenty-year-olds. Eight monks from the Jokhang and three from the small Nechung monastery had joined them.

This time, too, the demonstration had begun at nine in the morning.

The demonstrators had walked the Barkor circuit with the Tibetan flag and cries of 'Bod Rangzen'. Over one hundred Tibetans had joined the procession. As they walked around Barkor for the fourth time, the police took action.

The monks were beaten and arrested. Thirty civilians were rounded up along with them. They were all taken to the Barkor Square police station.

Over three thousand Tibetans gathered in front of the police station.

The clash was brutal and inevitable.

Since there were a few foreign tourists in Tibet at the time, the news of the 1st October protest demonstration in Lhasa reached first the Indian and then the international news agencies.

On Monday 5th October I went to the Dalai Lama's Office at 10, Ring Road in New Delhi.

I asked to speak to Tashi Wangdi, then Information and International Relations Minister of the Tibetan government in exile.

Tashi Wangdi was forty years old. A short black beard framed his face, marked by the tension of the last few days.

It had been the monks who had organised the two protest marches in Lhasa. I asked Tashi Wangdi the reason why.

He replied: 'Buddhism is at the centre of every Tibetan's life. Lamas and monks have always had a very important role in our society, in spiritual as well as administrative life. Lamas and monks are not just people who withdraw to the mountains to meditate. The identity of Tibet and the people's suffering are very important to them. They are very politically conscious. There is another consideration to be made. It is easier to get organised in the monasteries. If one wishes to organise a protest march it's easy to find a way to do it. If we take a closer look at the two demonstrations in Lhasa, we can see how, in both cases, they started with monks walking around the Barkor circuit. For the faithful, walking clockwise around a sacred path — doing "khorra," as we Tibetans call it — is a way to accumulate merit. But while praying, prostrating oneself, spinning prayer wheels, lighting incense and making offerings to monasteries are all individual actions, the khorra is a collective ritual. One circles a sacred building together with others. This is why it was easy for the monks in Lhasa to add political significance to the khorra.'

Tashi Wangdi informed me that the Dalai Lama would be holding a press conference in McLeod Ganj on Wednesday 7th October. He invited me to attend.

Then he gave me a photocopy of an important document that had just arrived at the Delhi office. It was the evidence that the forty-five foreign tourists in Lhasa on the 1st October 1987, the day of the second anti-Chinese demonstration, had provided.

The document had been hand-written by several people.

It read: 'Nine o' clock in the morning, 1st October. Thirty monks followed by a large group of the faithful have been walking around the Barkor shouting slogans and waving Tibetan flags. Sixty people have been arrested. They have been dragged into the police station a stone's throw from the Jokhang. Chinese policemen are photographing the crowds from the roof of the police station. A thousand people have gathered in front of the police station. There are two thousand in the nearby Barkor Square. The police have called for reinforcements. Forty plainclothes policemen with truncheons hidden in their sleeves are trying to merge into the crowd. A group of women and some boys start throwing stones at the guards in front of the station. The plainclothes police try to drag some Tibetans away. They are spotted, punched and made to run away from the demonstrators. At nine forty five the hail of stones gets thicker. The soldiers, plainclothesmen and police photographers are forced to beat a retreat.

'There has been no firing until now. Some of the women begin to pull up the cobblestones on the road. They use their aprons to collect stones to throw at the police. The monks beat up the police photographers on the Jokhang roof. A Chinese soldier running from the crowd loses his rifle. A few boys pick it up. They break it to pieces on the cobbles. The same boys throw the escaping soldier's cap with the red star in the air several times. A woman runs across the street to where seven police jeeps are parked. With the help of three youngsters she shatters the windscreens of the vehicles. She calls to the others. The jeeps are turned over. Someone sets them on fire. After about ten minutes the jeeps blow up. Four fire tankers arrive, escorted by army soldiers. The crowd pushes them back. The women encourage people to set fire to the police station door. The men race towards it with wooden boards and tins full of kerosene. An old man carefully rolls up a hose abandoned by the firemen. Then he throws it into the middle of the flames.

'At ten-thirty the first rifle shots are heard. People think they are firecrackers being set off in a nearby school. Three monks, one of them older than the others, lead the charge on the police station. Other shots can be heard from inside the police station. Ten minutes later the elderly monk[1] comes

1. The 'old monk' who had led the assault on the Barkor police station was called Champa Tenzin. He was 45 years old in 1987. Five years later, on the 22nd February

running out of a side door. His clothes and hands are burnt. The crowd cheers him. A little later, the monks arrested during the course of the morning escape from the doors and windows of the building, which has gone up in flames. The gunshots are more frequent now. Four wounded people are carried away. A rocket hits a youth of sixteen on his head. He dies. Three monks, two from the Sera monastery and one from Nechung, are killed as they escape from the police station. Not far away a man collapses to the ground in a puddle of blood. He dies on the spot. An eight-year-old child receives a bullet in his back. People help him. But there's no hope for him either. By three in the afternoon all the Chinese soldiers have deserted the police station. The fire continues to rage. The people begin their ransacking.'

After my conversation with Tashi Wangdi, I went to a little travel agency in Lajpat Nagar. I would have to get a train to Pathankot that very night so as to be able to get to the Dalai Lama's press conference on time.

There were a great many Indian journalists in McLeod Ganj on Wednesday 7th October, and representatives of nearly all the international press in Delhi.

Someone asked the Dalai Lama: 'Do you feel that the current protest demonstrations mark a turning point in the Tibetan struggle?'

The Dalai Lama replied: 'The turning point was the Lhasa insurrection of the 10th March 1959. The current demonstrations are nothing but a continuation of that protest. Tibetans are suffering under the Chinese colonial regime. It is their right to

---

1992, he was found dead in his cell inside the Jokhang. He had a rope around his neck and his face was covered with blood. The police said it was suicide. The monks accused the Chinese of having murdered him.

The other end of the rope was tied to one leg of his bed. The monks said it would have been impossible for him to hang himself in that position. Besides, they added, if he had strangled himself he would not have bled so much.

rebel.'

'The Chinese authorities accuse you of fomenting rebellion.'

'The Chinese always look for a scapegoat. There was immense destruction in Tibet during the Cultural Revolution. Ever since, the Chinese have been blaming the "Gang of Four". Now these spontaneous protest movements are taking place because of the repression, discontent and suffering of the Tibetan people. The Chinese don't want to admit it and, once again, they are looking for someone to blame.'

'Do you envisage more demonstrations of this kind?'

'The protest will continue until the cause of discontent has been removed.'

After the press conference, I returned to the McLeod Ganj bazaar. Demonstrators had blocked Temple Road. That 7th October was the thirty-seventh anniversary of the Chinese invasion of Tibet.

Two thousand Tibetan refugees were sitting on the road in front of the small McLeod Ganj temple. They were protesting silently. On their signboards was written: 'We do not have a homeland; the Chinese have taken it away from us.' 'Free nations everywhere in the world: Help us.' 'They have destroyed our houses and ransacked our temples.' 'Tibet for the Tibetans'. 'Out of our land, yellow pigs.'

An old lady with a rosary in her hand rose to her feet. "Down with the Chinese,' she shouted in a reedy voice. 'Freedom for political prisoners in Lhasa,' the crowd echoed. Some young women were in tears. 'Stop executions in Tibet,' the Tibetan Youth Congress militants shouted.

It was two men being executed that set off a new wave of protest in the 'Land of Snows.'

On Thursday 27th September 1987, three days after the

Dalai Lama's speech to the American Congress, the Communist Party of the Autonomous Region of Tibet organised a big 'thamzing', a struggle session, in the Lhasa stadium.

The 'work units' and 'neighbourhood committees' forced over fifteen thousand Tibetans to take part. The entire staff of the Communist Party was present. The deputy mayor of Lhasa spoke on everyone's behalf. 'We must defend the unity and the stability of the country,' he said. 'We must follow the four cardinal Party principles: the leadership of the Communist Party; the path that leads to socialism; Marxism-Leninism and the ideas of Mao Zedong; the dictatorship of the proletariat.'

The thamzing ended with eleven Tibetans being condemned—three to death and eight to maximum imprisonment. Two Tibetans, Kalsang Tashi and Migmar Tashi, were executed in the stadium in front of fifteen thousand spectators. A third, Sonam Gyaltsen, was killed the next day.

A witness recounted: 'The police tied the prisoners' wrists behind their backs. Their sentences were read out loud. With a rope tied to a beam the police pulled up two of the three who had been condemned to death by their wrists. They pulled up the rope until their elbows snapped. Then, with a pistol shot on the back of their heads, the two were executed.'

The victims' families had to reimburse the price of the bullets before the Chinese authorities would allow them to take away the bodies.

Once, during the thamzings, things had been even worse. The condemned person had his tongue cut out before being executed. That way they could prevent him shouting 'Bod Rangzen,' 'Free Tibet,' before he died.

Sum: Three (March 1988)

Tsongkhapa, the founder of the Gelug tradition, had started the big Monlam Prayer Festival.

During Monlam, the monks would pray for the well-being of all living creatures.

The festival traditionally lasted three weeks. Over twenty thousand monks from Ganden, Drepung and Sera, the three great Gelug monasteries of Lhasa, would take part.

Tens of thousands of pilgrims from all over Tibet would come to the capital for the occasion.

After the 1959 Lhasa insurrection the festival was abolished. It was only in 1986 that the Chinese cautiously permitted a renewal.

It was evidence of the Chinese Communist Party's 'new direction' in Tibet.

The new version of the festival was to last only ten days.

In 1988, there was a lot of tension in Lhasa on the eve of Monlam.

Many of the Tibetans arrested during the riots of the 27th September and the 1st October the preceding year were still in prison. The monks of Ganden, Drepung and Sera threatened to boycott the festival. They demanded the release of all political prisoners, especially Yulu Dawa Tsering.

Geshe Yulu Dawa Tsering was fifty-three. He was a graduate in Buddhist philosophy. He had been condemned to twenty years in prison for having taken part in the 1959 Lhasa insurrection. He had been freed in 1979.

In 1984, when the University of Tibet was opened in Lhasa, he was assigned the Buddhist philosophy chair. The Chinese sought thereby to make him a sympathiser of the regime.

Instead, Yulu Dawa Tsering continued to support Tibet's right to independence. On the 26th December 1987 he was arrested once again. The Chinese accused him of 'counter-revolutionary propaganda.' They said it was he who had fomented the protest demonstrations of September and October 1987.

The monks of the three great Lhasa monasteries were now asking for him to be released.

In reply the Chinese administration threatened to expel all the 'irregular' monks from the monasteries. They meant the young monks who had come to Lhasa for the Monlam festival without a stay permit.

A compromise was reached. The festival began as scheduled on the 24th February 1988. But only half the monks who had been invited took part.

The authorities' stand had been erected near Barkor, alongside the 'Sungchorawa', the place from which the Dalai Lama once traditionally delivered his New Year's Day sermon.

State television broadcast coverage of the festival all over Tibet.

On the 3rd March, the third from last day of Monlam, there had been a small upset. In the crowd at the festival was a monk from Drepung who had risen to his feet and shouted 'Bod Rangzen' in the direction of the authorities' stand. The other monks had immediately hushed him and made him sit down again.

On the 4th March the monks who had successfully completed their studies in Buddhist philosophy were given their degrees.

The 5th March was the last day of Monlam.

A statue of Maitreya, the Future Buddha, was carried in a procession atop a truck around the Jokhang.

At nine forty-five in the morning the truck returned to the main entry of the cathedral.

The statue of Maitreya was put back inside the cathedral. The Monlam festival was about to end.

It was then that a group of monks from Ganden started running in the direction of the authorities' stand. They were shouting slogans. They were particularly upset with Ragdi, the deputy secretary of the Communist Party of the Autonomous Region of Tibet.

Ragdi had visited the various monasteries in person to persuade them to take part in the festival.

Now the monks asked him to free the political prisoners and, in particular, Yulu Dawa Tsering.

The tone of the protest became heated almost immediately. Then the situation degenerated.

This is how a monk from Drepung who later escaped to India told the story: 'On the 5th March, at the start of the protest, the monks loudly asked that Yulu Dawa Tsering be freed. "You promised us you would free him," they shouted. A Chinese public administration official told the monks to be silent. Then he took a stone and flung it at them. The monks picked up the stone and threw it back at the authorities. At that moment, someone in the stand fired a revolver shot. A Tibetan - a Khampa - fell to the ground, dead. The crowd began to shout "Bod Rangzen." Led by Ragdi, the authorities ran away. They found refuge inside the Jokhang on the premises of the Buddhist Association, a governmental institution. Meanwhile, the crowd was carrying the body of the dead Khampa in procession around the Barkor circuit. The police called for reinforcements. The men of the People's Armed Police (PAP) rushed to the spot. They had stones thrown at them by Tibetans on the roofs of the Barkor houses. The demonstrators went around the Jokhang circuit a third time. There were over two thousand of them. The head of the procession could see its tail.'

Having finished the third round of the Barkor, to avoid being arrested the monks sought refuge inside the Jokhang. Ragdi and other Chinese Communist Party members were also within the cathedral, barricaded inside the Buddhist Association offices.

Ragdi and his companions were only freed two hours later

by PAP men. As people hooted, they climbed out of a window on the second floor of the cathedral with the help of a ladder.

Another monk told what happened inside Jokhang when it was stormed by the People's Armed Police. 'A big crowd had surrounded Jokhang. The doors had been barred from the outside and it was no longer possible to get out. I climbed on to the roof. There were a lot of monks there, throwing stones at the police and their vehicles. I joined them. Suddenly the PAP men burst into the cathedral from the roofs of the nearby houses. They were wearing steel helmets and gas masks. They began to hit the monks savagely. They hit them with nail-studded sticks and iron bars. They kicked them. The monks who had been hit collapsed on the floor. The PAP men tied their hands behind their backs with rope. Then they dragged them away. There were about two hundred monks inside the Jokhang. The rumour began to spread that most of them had been killed. I myself saw a dead monk. I knew him. He was from Nakchu province. He had been beaten to death with an iron bar. He lay there in the first floor gallery in a pool of blood. His skull had been bashed in. I saw the PAP men throw a monk from Ganden from the roof of the Jokhang into thin air.

'It was suffocating because of the tear gas. The monks tried to hide anywhere they could. When the policeman found them they herded them into the ground floor courtyard and thrashed them. I found myself on the roof of the Sheri building. When I saw the PAP men arrive, I threw myself off. I came to in hospital, guarded by three armed men.'

A third eyewitness, a monk from Ganden, recounted what he saw outside the cathedral. 'No one knew how many monks had been killed inside the Jokhang. I saw PAP men fling a monk from Sera from the cathedral roof. The body landed on the cobblestones with a huge thud. The monk's head was shattered, but he was still alive. We carried him to a nearby house. He was in agony for hours. He died towards midnight. That same night we called four monks to recite the funeral prayers. A little later the police arrived. They arrested the four monks. The next day we cremated the body of the monk from Sera. On the 5th March 1988, at least sixteen Tibetans died in clashes with the police.'

The monks who had been taken to hospital were put behind bars as soon as they got well.

For several weeks after that, many Tibetans were sent to jail. The police would take them from their houses at night. They were the 5th March demonstrators, identified by the photographs the police had taken.

In jail, dogs mauled the prisoners. They were beaten, subjected to electric shocks, tied to the rafters and left hanging for hours.

Immediately after they were arrested, the demonstrators were taken to the Gurtsa and Sangyib prisons.

Gurtsa was an 'interrogation centre' managed by the Lhasa Security Bureau. Sangyib was a 'camp of reform through work' (*lao gai*).

Once their sentences had been pronounced, the prisoners were transferred to Drapchi prison to serve their terms.

***

At the end of our meeting in the Lung-ta Building in McLeod Ganj, Yeshe Togden, the president of the Gu-Chu-Sum, gave me a small bracelet.

The political prisoners in Drapchi prison had made it with white and black wool. The bracelet was in the same colours as the 'zi', the Tibetan auspicious stones.

Dalai Lama

5th October 1989: The Tibetan community in India is celebrating. The 5 p.m. news on the radio has just announced that the Dalai Lama has won the Nobel Peace Prize. The reason: 'For having consistently opposed the use of violence in the struggle for the liberation of Tibet.'

***

The envelope bearing the letter from the Department of Information and International Relations had the logo of the Tibetan government in exile embossed on it in red ink.

The letter contained the date and time of our meeting.

The Dalai Lama had consented to give me an exclusive interview shortly before leaving for Oslo to receive his prize.

When I left Delhi it was already evening.

I travelled all the way across town in an Ambassador taxi.

The traffic was in turmoil, the noise deafening.

At the traffic lights, the metal flanks of the buses seemed to hum impatiently.

Dim lights inside the coaches lit the passengers' dark faces.

When the lights changed to green the traffic roared forward again. Trucks, buses, cars, taxis, three-wheeler auto-rickshaws and motorcycles all left behind a choking black cloud.

Old Delhi Railway Station resembled a leper hospital. Tens of people lay on the ground. They were wrapped in rags and blankets, trying to shield themselves from the cold.

An unlit iron bridge took me to Platform 1A opposite the entry. An excited, noisy crowd was waiting for the train.

There were several soldiers. They had faces with Mongol features and wore camouflage gear.

There were elderly nihang, warrior followers of Guru Gobind, with white beards and daggers.

There was a female sadhu dressed in saffron carrying a bag on her head.

The loud conversations on the platform were drowned by the shouts of hawkers. They invited people to buy their goods - newspapers, biscuits, fruit, locks and chains.

A female voice on the loudspeaker announced that the Kalka Mail would be forty-five minutes late. 'The inconvenience caused is deeply regretted.'

Another loudspeaker announcement: 'Do not touch objects left unguarded in the station.' And then another: 'Do not accept food offered by strangers.'

The train arrived over an hour later. The word 'Kumaon' was written in chalk on several wagons. They were reserved for soldiers on their way to Kashmir.

I was in carriage number 14023. I found my seat easily.

I had all night to think of the questions I wanted to ask the Dalai Lama.

I got down at Pathankot. It was early in the morning. The town was grey and dusty. The roads were full of potholes. There were heaps of garbage everywhere. I got into a Maruti van and left immediately for McLeod Ganj. After crossing the bridge over the Beas river, I entered Himachal Pradesh.

The scenery suddenly became more peaceful. It was coloured the emerald green of wheat fields, the yellow of mustard, the lilac of wildflowers. There were rivers, valleys, hills and fruit trees. The snow-covered peaks of the first Himalayan spurs were visible in the distance. The inferno of Delhi was a long way away.

In McLeod Ganj I booked into the Hotel Tibet.

There was a photocopied notice Scotch-taped on the inside of my door. It read:

HOUSE GUESTS

McLeod Ganj is a land of Monkies who like to fiddle with any goods or eatable which is always within their reach.

Therefore it would be good if the Guests close down all the windows before leaving out from their respective rooms in order to avoid finding their goods all in a mess.

The gate of the Dalai Lama's residence was in front of Tsuglagkhang, the Central Cathedral. An Indian policeman frisked me.

A member of the Central Tibetan Administration read the letter from the Department of Information and checked my papers. He led me to a round waiting room.

He returned almost immediately. 'Please come,' he said.

I walked up a small slope and reached the top of a little hill. I went through a garden with flowers in full bloom and found myself in front of a modest single-storied building.

The Dalai Lama was waiting for me on the veranda.

He greeted me with a smile and a handshake.

I offered him the white silk scarf I had bought for a few rupees in the McLeod Ganj bazaar.

We went into the meeting room. It was simply furnished. There were a couple of sofas and two armchairs and a few thangkas hanging on the walls.

I asked the Dalai Lama, 'What do you consider peace to be?'

He replied, 'Peace is not only the absence of war. It is much more than that. It is true that war brings suffering and destruction. But the mere absence of war is not enough. The final aim of peace is the happiness of all human beings. This must be our objective.'

'Immediately after the Nobel Prize was announced, you

once again accused China of genocide...'

'Tibet's main problem today is the population transfer. Hundreds of thousands of Chinese are transferred from China to Tibet. We find ourselves facing a real demographic aggression. If this process goes on, soon Tibet will no longer be the land of Tibetans. It will become just one more region populated by a Chinese majority and dominated by Chinese culture.

'In the province where I was born, there are 700,000 Tibetans and two and a half million Chinese today. If this process extends into all of Tibet, it will be a tragedy not only for us, but for the whole world. An ancient culture will vanish forever.

'Then there is the language problem. Despite the official statistics saying the opposite is true, Tibetan is no longer seriously taught in schools. Chinese is given exclusive preference.

'Finally, there is the problem of birth control. The Chinese admit that they lack manpower in Tibet. Yet Tibetans are subjected to strict birth control.'

'In what way?'

'Not long ago, once again in the Amdo region, Chinese officials told the Tibetan nomads of the arrival of a good doctor to cure people. When the medical team arrived, all the women had to undergo forced sterilisation. Even fourteen and fifteen year old girls were not spared. This can no longer be defined birth control. Hence I speak of genocide.'

'Some Tibetans, especially the younger ones, criticise your political choices. They say that non-violence doesn't lead anywhere...'

'It's not only a generational question. There are also many older Tibetans who think that violence is the only efficient form of struggle. But I don't agree. I believe that kindness and a good heart are the real features of human nature. Perhaps we can solve one problem through violence. But we would sow the seeds for the growth of new problems. What is obtained through violence cannot last long. It can only have negative consequences...'

'You have said that you may be the last Dalai Lama of Tibet. Why is that?'

'According to Chinese propaganda, since the so-called "liberation" Tibetans are happy and Tibet has started on the road to progress. They say the only danger is the Dalai Lama. Having lost his earlier privileges, he is plotting to restore the old feudal regime.

'My response to this accusation is that the tradition of the Dalai Lama might well come to an end. The survival of this institution will depend entirely on the will of the Tibetan people. If, in the future, the circumstances are such that a Dalai Lama is no longer necessary, the institution will automatically come to an end.'

'Once you are dead, the Chinese could pick out any child and say, "This is the new Dalai Lama." Do you think this is possible?'

'It is possible. They have already done it to a certain extent with the Panchen Lama, who died this year in January. The Chinese have openly said that they want the reincarnation of the next Panchen Lama to take place within the borders of the People's Republic of China.

'There is no doubt that the Chinese are waiting impatiently for me to die...(*laughs*). In any case I have already said that, if I were to die now and the Tibetans wanted another reincarnation of the Dalai Lama, they will find him among Tibetans and not in the hands of the Chinese. The true scope of reincarnation is to carry forward the work done in one's previous life...'

'You are simultaneously the spiritual leader and the political head of the Tibetans. How do you reconcile religion and politics?'

'The two things are not contradictory. I believe that our struggle also signifies a lot on the spiritual level. I consider all my activities part of my religious practice. If your motivation is sincere and compassionate, then all your activities become spiritual.

'But, if I can return one day to a Tibet that is finally free, I have already decided that I will not take up any kind of leadership. I will live as a simple Buddhist monk.'

'How do you envisage Tibet in the future?'

'No Tibetan wants to return to the old regime. At the beginning of the 1960s the Tibetan government in exile tried to draw up an outline of Tibet's future political system. But it was only a trial. It is the Tibetan people who will decide.'

'What is your view of the events in Tiananmen Square last June?'

'They will become very important in the long term. As a result of the student revolt, people both inside the People's Republic of China and the rest of the world have understood the real character of the Communist Chinese regime. If Communism still had another thirty years to go in China, after Tiananmen its chances of survival have been halved...'

'Communism is collapsing everywhere in the world. Does this have anything to do with the Buddhist law of causality?'

'Certainly. Terror has always been one of the most efficient ways to govern. Communism — with its rigidity and regime of fear — has always made good use of it. After the Soviet and then the Chinese revolutions, the terror continued. The rigidity of the Communist system blocked the creative qualities of human nature from developing. The result has been stagnation in every field — financial, scientific, technological, educational and cultural. For sixty years the Soviet Union managed to cover it all up with lies. But you can't keep lying...'

'What contradictions do you see in the materialistic West?'
'The West has one guarantee against the breakdown of existing political systems — freedom. If there is freedom of thought and speech, one can find remedies when things go wrong. It is equally possible to see what isn't working and to try to fix it.

'It is true that in Western countries there is a lot of emphasis on material growth. A materialistic ideology is dominant everywhere. But things are changing. Young people today are peaceable and ecologically minded. Thinkers, scientists and individuals are getting increasingly interested in the inner world, spirituality and the search for moral values.'

'Is there a link between spirituality and ecology?'
'Yes. When I talk of spirituality I don't mean religion. I mean the basic human values — compassion, love, forgiveness, non-violence. These qualities are not the monopoly of religion. Religion can help to develop them. When a child is born it is free from any kind of dogma or religion. But from its very first day of life it expresses affection and love. It is not exempt from these human qualities.'

'Coming back to ecology...'
'True compassion is not only a feeling of pity or the bonds of affection. Compassion means being concerned for others. The future generations will be part of our own humanity. We

must respect their rights. We must safeguard the planet for them too. It is this altruistic attitude that links spirituality and ecology.'

'What is Tibet's situation from the environmental point of view?'

'Tibet is a country of exceptional natural beauty. The Chinese have destroyed almost all its forests. Its fauna too is nearly extinct.

'We know that there is a lot of military-related industry around the Kakonor lake. One of these factories produces nuclear weapons. People have seen deformed animals in the area...

'Besides, we hear news that the Chinese want to turn Tibet into a dumping ground for radioactive waste. It would appear that the Chinese have offered the government of the so-called Autonomous Region of Tibet a reward of three million yuan for storing radioactive waste on its territory.'

'The justification offered by the Nobel Committee for the prize you are being awarded recognises your "having developed a philosophy of peace from a great reverence for all things living". This is what Buddhism teaches.'

'Man often has something to learn from even the lowest animals — insects, bees, ants...These animals have a strong sense of responsibility. When we observe bees, we realise that they work together on an extremely co-operative basis. They have no religion, constitution or laws that force them to stay together. Yet, because of their nature and their way of life, if they do not work together, they cannot survive.

'The survival of our planet and our whole universe also depend on this kind of cooperation. We humans think we are superior. Instead, we sometimes reveal ourselves to be inferior to these tiny insects.'

'What can Buddhism offer people today?'

'Buddhism is a very sophisticated philosophy that gives rationality a great deal of importance. It can help to develop an open mind and a flexible attitude. People are slaves to dogma far too often, and this can lead to situations that are hard to control. But if one follows a middle way, one's opinions are more balanced. A lot of people might find this theory of relativity and interdependence useful.'

'What does Buddhism teach?'

'Buddhism teaches that kindness, altruism and a good heart are the sources of any kind of happiness - not only in religious terms but in daily life as well. So we have to ask ourselves if it is possible for us to increase compassion and altruism - that is, whether it is possible to increase these qualities in our own minds while putting a stop to anger, hate and envy.

'From my limited experience I can say that one can modify one's own mind as a result of constant training. It is possible to strengthen our positive behaviour and reduce the negative.'

'What is the biggest obstacle to being compassionate?'

'Selfishness — the behaviour of those who seek benefit for themselves without thinking of others.'

'How can we eliminate hate from our lives?'

'If we were to think about it very hard, we would understand that when our enemies do us harm, we should be grateful to them. It might seem paradoxical, but it is exactly at these times that we can put our patience to the test. In this way we can accumulate merits and receive their benefits. Our enemy, on the other hand, will have to pay for the wrong he has done. It is as if he were sacrificing himself for us, entirely for our benefit. And this is why I can't resent even the Chinese...(*laughs*).'

The interview was over. The Dalai Lama whispered something into his secretary's ear. The man went out of the room and reappeared almost immediately. He bore a white silk scarf and a small envelope.

The Dalai Lama placed the votive scarf around my neck. There were the eight auspicious Tibetan symbols in filigree on the khata.

The small envelope contained a silver coin.

It had been minted in 1906.

On one side of the coin was written in Tibetan, 'Gaden Phodrang (the Tibetan government) victorious in all directions.' There was a lotus on the other side.

The Dalai Lama asked me to accept the coin as a souvenir of the interview.

I thanked him.

'Thank you, thank you,' Tenzin Gyatso replied, and accompanied me to the veranda.

Before leaving, I asked the fourteenth Dalai Lama of Tibet how he would like to be remembered.

'As a human being who often smiled,' was his reply.

Panchen Rinpoche

That morning Choekyi Gyaltsen, the tenth Panchen Lama, was a happy man. His lifelong dream was perhaps about to come true.

He was back at his monastery, Tashilhunpo, in Shigatse, Tibet once more.

He had brought with him five metal boxes containing the bones of the Panchen Lamas who had preceded him. During the Cultural Revolution, the Red Guards had destroyed the stupas in which they were kept.

The bones had been thrown into the dust, among the rubble. But they had been secretly salvaged. Since 1980 the Panchen Lama had kept them safe in his house in Beijing.

Now the Chinese had built a funeral shrine to make amends.

For the government in Beijing it was a good opportunity for some propaganda. The funeral monument was tangible proof of the religious freedom the Chinese Communist Party conceded the Tibetan people.

The stupa was an impressive twelve metres high. It was located inside a building that was a good thirty-two metres in height.

It was the 22nd January 1989. It was cold. But the sun shone in the cobalt blue sky above Shigatse.

The cloister of the Tashilhunpo monastery was crammed with monks.

At a quarter past nine in the morning the Panchen Lama arrived.

Two monks preceded him, bearing silver trumpets decorated with yellow, red and blue woollen ribbons.

Choekyi Gyaltsen's imposing bulk was wrapped in a lemon yellow brocade chuba. Next to him, a monk held a parasol of the same colour high up on a pole.

The Panchen Lama swung his arms as he walked.

There was an ironic smile on his lips.

That day he was getting his revenge. He thought of the nine years he had spent in prison, and the 'struggle sessions' to which the Red Guards had subjected him.

Making his way through two rows of bowing monks with white silk khatas in their hands, the Panchen Lama climbed the steps leading to the entrance of the funeral shrine. He prostrated thrice on the ground after having raised his joined hands first to his forehead, then to his mouth and then to his heart.

There were the boring official speeches. The first to speak was Hu Jintao, secretary of the Communist Party of the Autonomous Region of Tibet. Then it was the Panchen Lama himself. His speech was rhetorical and servile — or at least that was how the Hong Kong newspaper *Ta Kung Pao*, which supported the Beijing government, put it. 'The rebuilding of this magnificent edifice shows the correctness of the Chinese Communist Party's position vis-à-vis religion and the various minorities,' the Panchen Lama was claimed to have said. 'This monument is also proof of the Han and Tibetan people's unity, as well as the patriotism of Tibet's religious population.'

But during another official speech in Shigatse the next day, Monday 23rd January, the Panchen Lama abandoned rhetoric and diplomacy. The *People's Daily* carried his words on its front page: 'There has undoubtedly been progress in Tibet from the liberation to today. But the price the Tibetans have paid has been higher than the benefits they have received.'

His words hurt the top brass of the Communist Party. Throughout the speech, Hu Jintao and his deputy Mao Rubai remained motionless, as if they had been turned into pillars of salt.

At Tashilhunpo, the festivities continued in the days that followed.

On the evening of the 27th January there was a big celebration. All the people who had saved the relics of the Panchen Lama from the iconoclastic fury of the Red Guards twenty years earlier were present. The workers who had built the big stupa were there too.

There was a reception followed by songs and dances, Chinese as well as Tibetan.

At one in the morning the Panchen Lama informed his guests that he was tired. 'Carry on with the celebrations. I'm going to turn in,' he said.

Choekyi Gyaltsen read for about half an hour before going to bed. Then he asked his assistant Lobsang Tsultrim for another blanket.

When the assistant returned with the blanket, he found a cordon of plainclothes policemen in front of the Panchen Lama's room. Lobsang Tsultrim was sent packing.

At four in the morning on the 28th January (according to the subsequent official police version) the Panchen Lama experienced strong chest pains. He called a doctor. He was given some medication and went back to sleep. He woke up at 8 a.m. A doctor visited him once again. The Panchen Lama said he was feeling 'much better.' Five minutes later, he fell to the ground. He was dead.

His funeral chamber was set up inside the 'Dekyi Podrang,' the 'Palace of Happiness,' the Panchen Lama's official residence in Shigatse. The building was near the main gate of the Tashilhunpo monastery.

On the 3rd February every single one of the eight hundred monks in the monastery placed a white silk khata at the foot of the bier.

In an adjoining room thousands of Shigatse residents paraded, their eyes filled with tears, in front of a photograph of the deceased Panchen Lama. Thousands of yak butter lamps were lit to pay homage to his memory.

The corpse of the tenth Panchen Lama was embalmed. It was a complicated business. First the internal organs were removed. Then the body was covered with sandalwood oil, saffron, spices and salt and bound tightly in yellow silk cloth.

For five months the body remained this way.

When the bandages were removed the body had contracted noticeably. With golden purpurin they painted the face, the neck, the upper part of the chest and the hands. Finally the corpse was buried.

***

The Panchen Lama is Tibet's second spiritual authority after the Dalai Lama. Both belong to the Gelug tradition.

The Dalai Lama is the manifestation of Chenrezig, the Boddhisattva of Compassion.

The Panchen Lama is a manifestation of Amitabha, the Buddha of Infinite Light.

A special relationship links the two. It is the Dalai Lama's task to identify the child who is the reincarnation of the Panchen Lama, and keep an eye on him during his training. The Panchen Lama, in turn, chooses the reincarnation of the deceased Dalai Lama.

But there is a fundamental difference between the two. The Dalai Lama is at the top of the structure of Tibet's spiritual and temporal power. The Panchen Lama is only a spiritual authority. He comes second to the Dalai Lama.

The tenth Panchen Lama had been a controversial figure.

When, still a child, he was identified as the reincarnation of the preceding Panchen Lama, his 'labrang' (entourage) remained close to the Beijing government.

For this reason the Panchen Lama's labrang decided to carry on the antagonism that had historically existed between Tashilhunpo (the Panchen Lama) and Lhasa (the Dalai Lama).

It was in the interest of both Chiang Kai-shek's nationalist and Mao Zedong's Communist government to encourage this rivalry. Both backed the Panchen Lama so as to weaken the Lhasa government.

It was not until April 1952 that the young Panchen Lama, aged fourteen, set foot in Lhasa for the first time. He arrived with an escort of two Chinese People's Liberation Army battalions.

The Potala witnessed the first meeting between the fourteen-year-old Panchen Lama and the Dalai Lama, just three years older.

The meeting was very tense. It took place in the presence of about ten Chinese Communist Party members and high-ranking officials of the Liberation Army.

On the 6th June 1952 the Panchen Lama left for Shigatse. He reached his monastery, Tashilhunpo, on the 23rd June. Soldiers from the first battalion of Mao Zedong's Red Army set up their headquarters in the buildings just outside the monastery.

When the clash between Lhasa and Beijing reached the point of no return in 1959, Tashilhunpo stayed out of the contest.

After the Dalai Lama escaped to India, the Chinese needed a religious leader to replace him. They tried to turn the Panchen Lama into their puppet.

In 1960 the Panchen Lama visited the province of Qinghai. He was shocked by what he saw.

In October the same year he participated in the eleventh anniversary celebrations of the People's Republic of China in Beijing. He addressed the National People's Congress. He said: 'Tibet today is going through an extraordinary time. Production is flourishing in towns and in the countryside.' He was lying.

In 1961 and 1962, Choekyi Gyaltsen continued his travels through Tibet and southern China.

The Panchen Lama was convinced that Mao, Zhou Enlai and the Chinese Communist Party were well intentioned. It was the Party cadres and local members who were corrupt. They looked out for themselves without thinking of the good of the people. Things had to be rectified.

The Panchen Lama decided to write a lengthy report to the leadership of the Chinese Communist Party.

In May 1962, after having made many changes, he wrote the definitive version of the text. It was 70,000 Chinese characters long. He titled it 'A report on the suffering of the masses in Tibet and other Tibetan regions and suggestions for future work to the Central Committee through the respected Prime Minister Zhou (Enlai).'

When the Panchen Lama's entourage read the report they strongly advised him against presenting it.

Ngulchu Rinpoche, the Panchen Lama's teacher, was the most decided of all. 'It will only bring misfortune,' he said. He explained that Mao and Zhou Enlai knew perfectly well what the situation in Tibet was. If they really wanted to do something about it they certainly would not require a twenty-four-year-old's suggestions.

But the Panchen Lama didn't change his mind.

He presented the report.

In his text, the Panchen Lama strongly criticised Mao's 'Great Leap Forward' policy. While Party cadres were telling their superiors that 'production has largely overtaken the targets fixed by Communist Party officials,' workers in the countryside didn't have enough food to eat.

The Panchen Lama wrote, 'Working people say that one person gets a monthly grain ration of only 10 jin (one jin = 1/2 kg), but there are people in some areas that don't even get that much. After the communal canteens were set up...the health of the masses is getting weaker day by day...People have been dying in large numbers, catching a common cold or other very minor infections....in some areas, there have been cases of whole households starving to death. The mortality rate is critical.'

The Chinese Communist Party reacted very strongly to the Panchen Lama's *70,000-Character Petition*.

Mao Zedong called it 'a poisoned arrow.'

For the Chinese Communist Party the Panchen Lama had become 'a reactionary who defends the interests of the old society.'

He was subjected to thamzings, struggle sessions. He was placed in solitary confinement. He was made to study Mao's writings. He was asked to admit his mistakes.

In early 1964 he was given a last chance to mend his ways. He was asked to denounce the Dalai Lama in Lhasa during Monlam, the big Prayer festival, in front of 10,000 people. He was to describe him as 'a reactionary in the service of foreign powers.'

Instead the Panchen Lama said, 'Today, here in front of you all, I declare my absolute certainty that is Holiness the Dalai Lama will return to Tibet one day and seat himself once again on the golden throne that belongs to him. Long live His Holiness.'

The Communist Party officials present were livid.

For the Panchen Lama, that was it.

He was labelled a 'dangerous enemy of socialism.' The entire Tashilhunpo managing committee, starting with Ngulchu Rinpoche, was accused of being part of the 'traitorous gang led by the Panchen Lama.'

With the Cultural Revolution in 1966 the attacks on the Panchen Lama became more violent.

Every day he was subjected to thamzing. He was accused of having made people eat his excrement, passing it off as 'precious pills,' and having made the faithful drink his urine.

He was trussed up with steel wire. They spat in his face and smeared dung all over it. They pilloried him on the streets of Lhasa as Red Guards with loudspeakers pronounced him 'Tibet's biggest parasite and reactionary.'

He ended up in jail. Nearly all his collaborators were executed.

For years nothing more was heard of the Panchen Lama. Many thought he was dead.

During the long years he spent in prison he was placed in solitary confinement. He was only allowed to read the works of Marx, Lenin and Mao Zedong, as well as *Red Flag*, the Chinese Communist Party's propaganda magazine.

He was released from prison on the 10th October 1977.

Another eleven years went by before the 'anti-party element' stigma was finally lifted.

When the Panchen Lama got out of prison he was a broken man.

He met a Chinese woman named Li Jie. She was the niece of an ex-Kuomintang general. They decided to marry. They had a daughter.

After rehabilitation the Panchen Lama returned to active life. He went into business. He wanted to channel the profits into setting up institutions dedicated to Tibetan culture and language. He also wanted to rebuild many of the religious buildings the Chinese had destroyed during the Cultural Revolution. The Tashilhunpo stupa inaugurated five days before his death marked the apex of his work for Tibetan culture.

***

In the Indian state of Karnataka, the Tibetan community in exile had recreated its big monasteries — Ganden, Sera, Drepung and Tashilhunpo.

In the summer of 1994, five years after the death of the Panchen Lama, I decided to visit the Tashilhunpo monastery in southern India.

I wanted to speak to the lamas and monks who had known the tenth Panchen Lama.

I wanted to ask them who Choekyi Gyaltsen had really been. Was he the 'fat shopkeeper who sold his country to the Chinese,' as many people in Tibet and in India described him? Or was he 'a patriot' as the Dalai Lama and some of his closest collaborators thought? And more - how far along was the search for his new reincarnation?

It was not easy to visit Bylakuppe.

In early June I made a request to the Dalai Lama's office in New Delhi. I filled the required form.

'Don't mention the Panchen Lama,' Ogyen Wangyal, an employee of the office, advised. 'Jut write "tourism".'

He also told me that it took 'at least three months' to obtain authorisation.

I had almost forgotten about the request when I received a call from Mr. Wangyal at the end of August. 'The Indian government has authorised your visit,' he said cheerfully. 'But you have to leave immediately. The permit is only valid from the 1st to the 8th September.' There was no time to lose.

I decided to fly to Bangalore, then hire a car to travel the 220 kilometres from the capital of Karnataka to Bylakuppe.

From the plane window the rivers, overflowing as a result of an abundant monsoon, looked like so many mud-coloured puddles.

I reached Bangalore at nine in the morning. A car was waiting for me. It was a white, dented Tata Estate.

The driver was dressed in white too. He was a thin man with slender arms. He wore a marigold on a string around his right wrist.

Balaji, as the man was called, touched a statue of Ganesh on the dashboard of the car. He carried his folded hands to his forehead, bent his head reverentially and then turned the engine on.

It was a beautiful day. Trees that were hundreds of years old lined the road - banyans with silvery multiple trunks, neem, rain trees. The branches of the trees to the right often met overhead with those on the left. It felt a bit like going down the nave of a cathedral in a car.

There were peasants selling coconuts in small heaps by the side of the road.

The Tata Estate overtook a few farm carts with rubber tyres. Elegant zebus, their long horns curving slightly backwards, pulled the carts. There were little round brass bells on the tip of each horn.

We passed emerald rice fields and date palms with slim trunks.

A group of women and children were throwing water at the foot of a large banyan tree. It was their morning prayer.

Trucks loaded with sandalwood went by.

Earth, water, wood — everything in the area was rust coloured.

A long canal cut across the road.

Immediately after it a sign greeted us: 'MYSORE CITY CORPORATION WELCOMES YOU'.

Beyond the trees that lined the road the two high, pointed towers of the Cathedral of Saint Philomena could be seen. They looked like two big zebu horns.

We passed the cathedral. It was imposing. Arrogant. The small shops made of palm fronds at its base selling tea, fruit and coconuts seemed even tinier and more fragile in comparison.

We stopped in Mysore for the night and left again early next morning. The tropical light was superb, the colours brilliant.

We had breakfast at the Ruchi restaurant in Hunsur.

In this town, thousands of kilometres from the Himalayas, I saw my first Tibetans — two monks. A little later I saw a Tibetan woman as well. She was selling coloured wool pullovers on the pavement.

We went through Priyapatna. There was an increasing number of Tibetans among the crowd.

Another twenty kilometres and we were in Bylakuppe.

Bylakuppe was a small farming town. There were only a few shops. They had wooden walls and thatched roofs.

There were vans and scooter-rickshaws parked all along the main road. A signboard read 'Long live Indo-Tibetan friendship.'

There were over 30,000 Tibetans living in Bylakuppe. A narrow, dusty road led to the 'Old Camp' and the 'New Camp.' Maize was being cultivated in the corrugated land all around. There were few trees. Most of the Tibetans in Bylakuppe were farmers.

A rickshaw-load of monks went by. A garnet-red soutane fluttered from its window. A Tibetan girl in jeans rode past on a big motorcycle, her hair flying in the wind

The first monastery I came across was Namdoling. Sixteen high white stupas announced its presence from afar.

The monks of the Namdoling monastery belonged to the Nyingma tradition.

The Sera monastery was next.

At half past eleven in the morning, hundreds of monks were coming out of the refectory with bowls of lentils and slices of unleavened bread in their hands.

A monk showed me the road that led to the Tashilhunpo monastery.

I saw the monastery from a distance. It stood in the middle of some maize fields.

To reach the monastery I had to cross the Old Camp, the first Tibetan refugee camp in South India.

Someone had written 'Boycott Chinese goods' on a water tank.

Compared to the Namdoling and Sera monasteries, Tashilhunpo was small, poor and somewhat run-down. A low, whitewashed boundary wall surrounded it. Four red-painted wooden pillars propped up the ceiling of the assembly room veranda.

It was dark inside. There were photographs of the ninth and tenth Panchen Lamas on two pillars to the left and right of the throne.

There was a single thangka on the entry wall of the room. It had the monastery of Tashilhunpo in Shigaste in Tibet drawn on it. It looked like a bird's eye view of a small town. The Panchen Lama's palace, the temples, the churches and hundreds of monks' houses were visible.

The houses of the 150 monks of the Indian Tashilhunpo, on the other hand, were small and one-storied.

My presence caused no little surprise, and a few monks soon arrived.

Sonam spoke a little English and offered to be my interpreter.

Before he ran away to India, Tupten Nyendak lived in the Tashilhunpo monastery in Tibet. He recounted: 'Between 1960 and 1962 the Chinese confiscated all monastery farming land. After the farming communes were set up food got more and more scarce. It was during this period that both my parents died of hunger. People had to accumulate a certain number of 'work points' assigned by the Chinese in order to survive. Many people died because of too much hard work and too little food. That was the 'democracy' the Chinese Communists brought to Tibet.'

A young lama, Ngulchu Rinpoche, added: 'Panchen Rinpoche was not indifferent to the Tibetan people's suffering. He saw that people were punished for no reason. He saw that monasteries were being razed to the ground. That was when he wrote his *70,000-Character Petition* against the Beijing government. In reply the Chinese communists decided to kill him. So his spiritual teacher Ngulchu Rinpoche stepped in. He said Panchen Rinpoche was still too young. "If anyone has to be killed," he said, "it should be me, since I am his teacher." Panchen Rinpoche on the other hand, told the Chinese authorities that his teacher was not involved. It was he himself who had written the petition. He would have to be the one to pay. In the end the Chinese communists killed Ngulchu Rinpoche. Now I am his reincarnation.'

Sonam Gyalpo was a monk at the Tashilhunpo monastery in Tibet when, in January 1989, the tenth Panchen Lama died there. He escaped to India immediately after that. He said, 'On the evening of the 22nd January 1989, Panchen Rinpoche had organised a big party at Tashilhunpo. All those who had helped build the funeral monument to the deceased Panchen Lamas were there. There were the masons, the carpenters, the painters, and the engineers. The next day Panchen Rinpoche intended to take part in a prayer session at the monastery. We were all gathered in the assembly hall when we were suddenly given the news that Panchen Rinpoche was dead. Some immediately said the Chinese had kidnapped and taken him back to China. It was a terrible shock for all of us. Many fainted. Others beat their heads against the wall, so hard that it was stained with blood. We had seen Panchen Rinpoche in perfect health in the preceding days. So why, now that we saw him dead, had his flesh turned black? Many thought the Chinese had poisoned him. The day before he died, Panchen Rinpoche had spoken in Shigaste in front of Communist Party officials. He had criticised the Chinese harshly.'

The monks of the Indian Tashilhunpo continuously prayed for the new reincarnation of the Panchen Lama to be identified as soon as possible.

They had also begun building a 'palace.' They hoped that one day the eleventh Panchen Lama would come there to live.

***

A new power struggle between McLeod Ganj and Beijing had begun. Whose was the right to identify the new reincarnation of the Panchen Lama?

The Chinese Communist Party had placed a 'democratic managing committee' at the head of the few monasteries left in Tibet. In each monastery there were tens of informers ready to denounce any form of dissent.

In the Tashilhunpo monastery in Shigatse, Chadrel Rinpoche, a lama who had spent five years at the Chinese institute for Buddhist studies in Beijing, headed the 'Committee'.

On the 25th August 1989, Chadrel Rinpoche announced in Tashilhunpo that the Chinese government had officially nominated him in charge of the search for the new reincarnation of the Panchen Lama. Beijing had however fixed the rules of the game. There were five obligatory steps before the new Panchen Lama could be officially nominated:
1. The interpretation of mystic omens to identify children who were candidates.
2. Having the children undergo traditional tests such as recognising objects belonging to the previous Panchen Lama.
3. The consultation of oracles and soothsayers to confirm the final shortlist of candidates.
4. The drawing from the Golden Urn of the name of the chosen candidate by a Chinese government official,
5. The approval of this candidate by the government of the People's Republic of China.

The first three points were specified by the Tashilhunpo monastery, the last two by the Beijing government.

The Golden Urn for the draw of the new Panchen Lama's name had been given to Tibet two centuries previously by a Qing dynasty emperor. For the Chinese this was proof of Tibet's subjection to China even in religious matters.

On the 26th September 1992, Chadrel Rinpoche informed the Chinese news agency Xinhua that the first phase of the search for the Panchen Lama was over.

Thrice the lamas of Tashilhunpo visited the sacred Lhamo Latso lake. For days on end they noted the signs that appeared on the surface of the water.

The Dalai Lama also initiated the procedure to identify the eleventh Panchen Lama.

First of all he consulted the oracle of Nechung.

The oracle replied that the child had been born and that he could be found in Tibet.

In March 1991 the Dalai Lama requested the Chinese embassy in New Delhi to permit him to send a delegation to Tibet to consult the Lhamo Latso lake in its turn. The delegation would then assist the monks of Tashilhunpo in Tibet to prepare the final list of candidates.

The Beijing authorities made it known that there was no need for 'external interference' in the search for the new reincarnation of the Panchen Lama.

For two years there was no further contact between McLeod Ganj and Beijing.

In 1993 something new happened. It seemed that the two parties could reach a compromise.

On the 17th July Gyalo Thondup, the Dalai Lama's elder brother, met Chadrel Rinpoche in a hotel in the Chinese capital. The meeting took place in the presence of several officials of the United Front, the Chinese Communist Party branch that handles relations with non-governmental organisations.

Chadrel Rinpoche seemed very tense during the meeting. He asked for the Dalai Lama's collaboration in identifying the eleventh Panchen Rinpoche. Gyalo Thondup replied that he had requested the Beijing authorities to allow McLeod Ganj and Tashilhunpo to communicate with each other.

Gyalo Thondup returned to India feeling reasonably hopeful.

The Dalai Lama immediately invited Chadrel Rinpoche to McLeod Ganj. The invitation was made through the Chinese embassy in New Delhi.

On the 30th August 1993, the corpse of the tenth Panchen Lama, mummified in a sitting position and dressed in yellow brocade, was finally buried in Tashilhunpo in Tibet inside a funeral monument that had cost the Beijing government eleven million yuan.

During the ceremony, Luo Gan, general secretary of the governing body of the People's Republic of China, said the Beijing government had wanted, with this monument, to honour the deceased Panchen Lama for his contribution to 'safeguarding the unity of the Motherland.'

It had been almost a year since the meeting between Chadrel Rinpoche and Gyalo Thondup. The Dalai Lama had waited in vain for Chadrel Rinpoche's reply. The Beijing authorities had abruptly interrupted any contact between the two.

In August 1994 the government of the People's Republic of China peremptorily asked the Tashilhunpo monastery to speed up the identification of the new Panchen Lama. The announcement had to be made in March the following year at the very latest.

From India, the Dalai Lama said in an official communication that the search for the new Panchen Lama was an exclusively religious matter.

Once again McLeod Ganj and Beijing were on a collision course.

But despite Beijing's official ban, the Himalayas were not an insurmountable barrier to communication between the Tashilhunpo monastery in Tibet and the Dalai Lama in India.

Faced with the choice of loyalty to the Beijing authorities and the demands of his own conscience, Chadrel Rinpoche selected the second alternative.

He secretly contacted the Dalai Lama.

In January 1995, a Tibetan monk appeared at the Dalai Lama's headquarters in India. Visibly exhausted after a long journey, the man told the officials of the Tibetan government in exile that he had come to India illegally in order to personally deliver a letter to 'Gyalwa Rinpoche' (the Dalai Lama).

After a lot of insistence the monk managed his meeting. He personally consigned a long, narrow white envelope to the Dalai Lama.

Inside the envelope were colour photographs of about twenty Tibetan children. There was also a letter from Chadrel Rinpoche. The future Panchen Lama would have to be chosen from among these twenty children.

In his letter, Chadrel Rinpoche asked the Dalai Lama to make the final choice. The name would have to be communicated to him in secret. He would then try and get it accepted by the Chinese authorities.

The Dalai Lama got to work at once.

He studied the children's photographs for a long time. He read their stories, written in Tibetan by Chadrel Rinpoche, attentively.

Only three candidates remained in the contest.

Three balls, three and a half centimetres in diameter, were prepared from barley meal dough. They were put on a balance to make sure they all weighed exactly the same.

A small roll of rice paper with a candidate's name was inserted into each of the balls. The balls were then placed in a copper cup.

The Dalai Lama held the cup in his hands for a long time. Then, with a slight movement of his wrist, he made the balls roll around inside the cup. He made them roll faster and faster until one ball detached itself from the others and sprang out of the cup.

The Dalai Lama marked the fresh dough of the ball with a thin wooden stick. He put the ball back into the cup. He repeated the procedure. Once again a ball detached itself from the others. It was the same one as before.

The Dalai Lama flattened the barley meal dough between his fingers. He extracted the roll of rice paper and read the name of the candidate: Gedhun Choekyi Nyima.

He would become the eleventh Panchen Lama of Tibet, the living manifestation of the Buddha of Infinite Light.

It was the evening of the 25th January 1995.

A second monk immediately left for Tibet.

He was to consign the Dalai Lama's letter with the indication of the chosen child to Chadrel Rinpoche.

When Chadrel Rinpoche was given the result of the Dalai Lama's divination, he began the risky business of trying to convince the Chinese authorities.

He told the Chinese he had carried out the divination. He said the name of Gedun Choekyi Nyima had emerged beyond all doubt. He said there would be no need for the extraction of the name from the Golden Urn.

But the Chinese were adamant. The name of the new Panchen Lama had to be extracted through a draw from the Golden Urn given to Tibet by the Qing dynasty emperor.

The name of Gedun Choekyi Nyima therefore not only risked not being chosen, but also not even being part of the final lot to be placed in the Golden Urn.

In March 1995 Chadrel Rinpoche went to Peking. He was to take part in the eighth session of the Consulting committee for national policies. He used the occasion to try one last time to convince the Chinese authorities. He repeated that the choice of the new Panchen Lama had already been made. There was no need to resort to the Golden Urn.

But Chadrel Rinpoche came up against a tough opponent in the consulting committee. He too was a 'rinpoche,' a reincarnated lama. His name was Sengchen Rinpoche.

The Tashilhunpo monks didn't approve of Sengchen Rinpoche. He had left the monastery, got married and gone to live in Lhasa.

At the consulting committee meeting Sengchen Rinpoche said that, just as the 'ambans' (emperor's representatives) controlled the procedure for the election of the Panchen Lama and the Dalai Lama in the Qing emperors' time, the Beijing government had every right to impose the use of the Golden Urn for the nomination of the new Panchen Lama.

Chadrel tried desperately to substantiate his own theory. But it was clear by now that the Chinese wanted to impose the use of the Golden Urn at any cost in order to reaffirm their control of Tibet.

In McLeod Ganj the Dalai Lama too was under pressure. The monks of the Tashilhunpo monastery in Bylakuppe in southern India were insisting he make the name of the new Panchen Lama public knowledge. They said that if the Chinese did it, every Tibetan in Tibet and abroad would think the Dalai Lama had merely ratified the Chinese choice.

The Dalai Lama asked the Bylakuppe monks to be patient. He wanted to get Chadrel Rinpoche's reply first. If he announced the name without that reply, the chances of the Chinese accepting the new Panchen Lama might diminish considerably.

But events raced ahead.

In McLeod Ganj it came to be known that Chadrel Rinpoche was about to be excluded from the Panchen Lama nomination process. The Chinese were going to use the Golden Urn. In all probability the announcement of the name of the new Panchen Lama would be made on the 23rd May, the anniversary of the signature of the Seventeen-Point Agreement between China and Tibet.

So there was no time to be lost.

Sunday 14th May 1995 was the anniversary of the Buddha's birth. The Nechung oracle said it would be a propitious day to make the announcement.

On the morning of the 14th May a meeting was held in the hall of ceremonies in the Dalai Lama's residence. Lamas, monks, ministers and officials of the Tibetan government in exile took part.

The Dalai Lama arrived at 8.30. He seated himself cross-legged on a small throne. There was a big picture of the Buddha Shakyamuni behind him.

Tenzin Gyatso's forehead was covered in perspiration. A ceiling fan whirred silently above his head.

There was a small framed photograph of Gedhun Choekyi Nyima on the altar.

The Dalai Lama explained how he had arrived at his final choice. Then he put on a yellow silk beret with earflaps down to his shoulders. A sheet of A4 paper was given to each monk and dignitary. Together they recited the prayer for the Panchen Lama that the Dalai Lama had composed.

While the ceremony was taking place, the information department of the Tibetan government in exile put out a release signed 'Dalai Lama'. It read: 'It is with great joy that I am able to announce the new reincarnation of Panchen Rinpoche. I have recognised in Gedhun Choekyi Nyima, son of Konchok Phuntsog and Dechen Chodon, born on the 25th April 1989 in the district of Lhari in the povince of Nagchu, Tibet, the true reincarnation of Panchen Rinpoche.'

Late in the morning of the 14th May all the Tibetans in McLeod Ganj met in front of the new temple in the sacred circuit around the Central Cathedral and the residence of the Dalai Lama.

Juniper shoots were set alight in great burners. Clouds of white smoke rose into the sky. The Tibetan Children's Village band played the Tibetan national anthem as a Tibetan flag was hoisted on a high pole.

The Dalai Lama's release was immediately published by wire agencies all over the world. The Voice of America broadcast it in Tibetan so that people living in Tibet could hear it too.

Chadrel Rinpoche heard the announcement on his way back from Beijing. The Chinese authorities arrested him in Chengdu together with his secretary, a monk named Champa Chung-la.

Chadrel Rinpoche was accused of having 'betrayed the Motherland.' But in an official communication the Chinese Ministry of External Affairs said Chadrel Rinpoche was 'ill' and that he had been 'hospitalised to undergo the necessary cure.'

Meanwhile, in the Lhari district, Gedhun Choekyi Nyima, the six-year-old the Dalai Lama had recognised as the eleventh Panchen Lama, had disappeared. His father, mother and older brother had also vanished. Someone had seen the little family in Nagchu escorted by the police. Then they had been spotted in Golmud. Here they had been put on a Chinese aeroplane and all trace of the four had subsequently vanished.

Liberation Army soldiers immediately occupied Shigatse. The monks of Tashilhunpo were told that if they were found to be in possession of a photo of the new Panchen Lama or caught reciting the Dalai Lama's prayer for him to have a long life, they would be executed.

In Lhasa too government vehicles patrolled the streets. Any sort of gathering was forbidden. But a poster appeared on the walls of the capital. Regarding the nomination of the new Panchen Lama, it read: 'None of us will accept interference and political pressure on the part of these devils who think religion is a poisonous weed and believe that lamas and monks are just wolves in disguise.' The poster was signed 'The representatives of the Tibetan people.'

On the night between the 28th and the 29th November 1995, the Jokhang in Lhasa was under police control. Just past midnight, some monks appeared inside the cathedral with red signboards on their chests. They sat down in the near dark in front of the statue of Jowo Shakyamuni.

Facing the monks with their backs to the statue of the Buddha were Luo Gan, secretary general of the governing body of the People's Republic of China, and Gyaltsen Norbu, governor of the Autonomous Region of Tibet. Beside them sat other officials of the Chinese Communist Party in suits and ties.

A wooden table with the Golden Urn on it stood between the monks and the Party officials. The urn was about forty centimetres high. There was a finely chiselled dice box in its long neck.

Lama Tsering, the monk who had replaced Chadrel Rinpoche at the head of the democratic managing committee of the Tashilhunpo monastery, pasted the names of the three children who would participate in the 'lottery' on three ivory sticks.

Lama Tsering placed the ivory sticks in three small yellow silk bags. He inserted them into the dice box in the urn. He shook the dice box several times and slipped it into the neck of the Golden Urn once more.

Bomi Rinpoche, an important lama of the Gelug tradition, was invited to extract one of the three bags.

One bag was visibly longer than the others. It stuck a few centimetres out of the dice box of the urn.

Bomi Rinpoche chose that bag.

He handed it to Gyalsten Norbu, the governor of the Autonomous Region of Tibet.

'Gyaltsen Norbu,' the governor shouted, as all the other officials of the Communist Party clapped. The child who had won the draw had the same name as the governor.

The child immediately appeared from behind the scenes. He was already dressed as the Panchen Lama. He wore a yellow chuba and a pointed cap on his head with two cloth horns over his forehead.

The child was given the name Jetsun Lobsang Chamba Lhundrub Choekyi Gyalpo Pe Zangpa. As far as the Chinese were concerned, he was the eleventh Panchen Lama.

A week after the draw Gyaltsen Norbu was officially enthroned at the Tashilhunpo monastery in Shigatse, Tibet.

Four months later, in March 1996, the monks of Tashilhunpo in Bylakuppe, India organised a counter-ceremony- the symbolic enthronement of the child chosen by the Dalai Lama who had subsequently disappeared.

At eight in the morning a long procession passed an incomplete building. It was the 'palace' destined to host the eleventh Panchen Lama. The procession entered the courtyard of the monastery. It went forward slowly between two rows of bowing monks holding white silk scarves.

In the centre of the procession a monk held up a big framed photograph of Gedhun Choekyi Nyima.

The photograph was placed on the altar of the assembly hall. A monk poured hot tea into a silver cup. He placed the cup in front of the photograph of the eleventh Panchen Lama. The monks and inhabitants of the refuge camp of Bylakuppe offered little Gedhun Chokyi Nyima a white silk khata.

The child seemed to be looking back at them from his photo with an air of amazement.

***

In September 2000 I returned to Bylakuppe.

I met Sonam, the young monk who spoke some English, again. I asked him if I could visit the Panchen Lama's 'palace' that they had just finished building.

Sonam sent for the guard monk. A grey haired man arrived. He was short and thickset and had a good-humoured expression on his face.

A lane with a slight downward slope led to the entry steps of a modest two-storey building. The ground floor had the service areas. The first floor was the important one and one got there by climbing a narrow flight of stairs with a heavy wooden handrail.

A wide corridor ran parallel to the façade of the building on the first floor. At the end of the corridor was a small two-roomed apartment. There was a parlour with a couch covered in yellow brocade, an inlaid sandalwood table and a chest-of-drawers with a framed photograph of the eleventh Panchen Lama on it.

The adjoining room contained a bed, a wardrobe and a small altar. The curtains at the windows were dusty pink. A pearly, almost unreal light filtered through. Everything was clean. Everything was in order. It was all ready to receive Gedhun Choekyi Nyima, 'the world's youngest political prisoner.'

The grey-haired monk turned to me. His eyes were bright with tears.

'It's very beautiful,' I said, exaggerating a little.

The old guard looked like a worried uncle waiting for his nephew.

'Is there any hope?' I asked.

'Everything is harder now,' he replied. 'But we keep waiting for him.'

Dorje Shugden

4th February 1997. It was winter in McLeod Ganj and the wind came down from the mountains, slipping into the brick hovels. At six in the evening it was already dark.

At Dolma Chowk, six young Tibetans took the descending road that led to Main Temple. They walked fast, huddling together.

The shops were already closing. To the right, on the edge of the valley, were four rickety wooden cages, their small doors covered by thick metal nets. There were bloody hunks of meat hanging inside the cages. A man crouched nearby.

Solidly constructed shops flanked the road on the left. There was a recently built six-story edifice. It was already mildewed and dilapidated. It hosted various shops and restaurants. One of them, 'Ali Baba's Treasures', already had its shutters down.

The six young Tibetans spoke in low voices. One of them was wearing a black baseball cap. He had a khaki cloth bag slung over one shoulder.

With a sudden curve the road turned at a right angle. A man was putting his wares — potatoes, carrots, cauliflower and oranges — back into wicker baskets. Through the pine trees the feeble lights of the buildings grouped around the Main Temple could already be seen.

There had been the carcass of a dog at this exact spot a few days earlier. It had been thrown into the woods near the road. The dead dog had a bloated stomach. Its teeth showed through a partly open mouth. Half a dozen crows were hopping around near it, cawing excitedly.

There was a small crossroads at the end of Temple Road. The peanut seller who generally stood near the incense burner had already left.

Dinner over, the monks were gathered in the Buddhist School Café drinking cups of boiling-hot tea. The square in front of the Institute of Buddhist Dialectics was deserted.

The entrance pavilion of the Institute was a small two-storyed building with a corrugated tin roof. An outside staircase led to the monks hostel.

The director of the Institute lived in a sparsely furnished room on the first floor. He was talking to two young disciples, Lobsang Ngawang and Ngawang Lodoe.

'Why is it wrong to venerate Shugden?' asked Lobsang, the older disciple.

'We must differentiate between gods and spirits,' the venerable Lobsang Gyatso, the director of the Institute, replied. 'Gods are transcendent entities. Spirits, on the other hand, belong to this world. Divinities have the Buddha nature. Spirits are like our servants. We can propitiate them in return for small, immediate benefits. But we shouldn't adore them or take refuge in them as if they were the Buddha.'

He added, 'It's as if we were to give more importance to a prime minister's bodyguard than the prime minister himself.'

The two disciples smiled.

The small green gate that opened on to the square in front of the Institute was ajar.

The six young Tibetans looked around. There was no one there. They went in.

There was a sign hanging on the wall: 'No visitors are allowed inside the premises of the hostel after 8 p.m.'

The six youths climbed the stairs almost at a run.

When they came to the director's room, they knocked.

'Geshe-la,' said the youth wearing the black baseball cap.

At half past four on the morning of the 5th February Jampa,

a young novice, carried a glass of hot tea to the director of the Institute. A steel plate with an upturned edge served as a tray. The novice found the door ajar and a dim light coming from the room. Jampa knocked. There was no reply. He pushed the door open with a foot. For a few moments he stood transfixed.

When he regained control of himself he placed the tea tray on the ground. The glass tipped over. The novice ran to the hostel bathrooms. 'Go and see,' he said to the other monks who were having a wash. Then he buried his face in his hands.

A forty-watt lamp with a cane shade lit the little room.

Lobsang Gyatso, the director of the Institute, was lying on the floor in a pool of blood.

His mouth was open and his teeth were bared. His throat was cut.

A knife had been stabbed deep into his forehead near his eyes, shattering his skull. Another stab in the middle of his chest had cleaved his heart. He was clutching a khaki bag in his left hand.

The two young disciples were also dead. They too lay on the ground in pools of blood. They too had had their throats cut.

***

The venerable Lobsang Gyatso was 69 years old. He was a corpulent man. He had a shaven head, big ears and a small, flat nose. His face was full of wrinkles.

He was born in the village of Choochur in the district of Kongjo Rawa in the Kham region. His parents were farmers. They called him 'Drangte', meaning 'a fellow scavenged from the beggar's rubbish'. They called him that because they wanted evil and envious spirits to leave him in peace. When he was seven they sent him out to take the sheep and goats to pasture. He went on with this job until the summer he turned 12, when he managed to convince one of his maternal uncles to get him into a monastery. Here he learned a few prayers by heart and took part in some religious festivals. But his real job didn't change much. Now he herded yaks and dzomos, albeit dressed as a novice.

At seventeen, he began the Drepung curriculum of study. He was good at debates. He alternated long periods of study and moments of solitary contemplation in the caves above the monastery.

In 1959 he ran away from Chinese-occupied Tibet. He went to India in exile. He attended a refresher course for teachers organised by the Indian government. He learnt how lay schools worked. Until the early 1970s he taught in the Tibetan Homes Foundation School in Mussoorie. In 1973 he proposed the opening of a new university college to the Dalai Lama. Thus the Buddhist Dialectics School was created in 1974, later becoming the Institute of Buddhist Dialectics.

When the courses began there were twenty-five monks and a sole teacher. In a few years time the Institute of Buddhist Dialectics became one of the most successful institutions of the Tibetan community in exile. The ancient system of education was remodelled along the lines of modern Indian universities.

Lobsang Gyatso wrote a lot of books. From 1978 on his writings became increasingly critical of the 'old social order'. The more conservative factions — both religious and secular — of the Tibetan community in exile distanced themselves from the director of the Institute.

Lobsang Gyatso was mainly critical of the Shugden cult.

The devotees of this 'spirit' were particularly offended by an article the director of the Institute wrote against Trijang Rinpoche, a follower of Shugden, a man of religion respected by all and 'second tutor' of the Dalai Lama.

In January 1997, a month before his assassination, Lobsang

Gyatso had written a new series of articles against the Shugden cult. He had sent copies to several people at his own expense.

Hence his name ended up on a secret 'hit list' prepared by a group of Shugden worshippers active in Bylakuppe in southern India and the refugee camp of Majnu ka Tilla in Delhi.

***

Dorje Shugden, 'powerful lightning', was a guardian spirit of relatively recent origin in the Gelug tradition. Legend had it that he was the spirit of the 17th century monk Drakpa Gyaltsen.

Drakpa Gyaltsen was born into a noble family in 1619. As a child he had been one of the candidates to be the fifth Dalai Lama. But another candidate was chosen and Drakpa Gyaltsen was recognised as the incarnation of Panchen Sonam Drakpa, one of the third Dalai Lama's teachers.

As youngsters both the Dalai Lama and Drakpa Gyaltsen studied at the Drepung monastery, where heated rivalry arose among their respective followers.

Drakpa Gyaltsen became a famous academic. One day he challenged the Dalai Lama to a debate. After the debate ended, Drakpa Gyaltsen was murdered. But there was another version of events.

Many lamas, and the Tibetan government itself, were jealous of Drakpa Gyaltsen's fame and his ever-increasing number of followers. They decided to do away with him. But, as a result of the supernatural powers he had acquired through prayer and meditation, the monk caused their attempts to kill him to be made in vain.

In the end, however, tired of the conspiracies and intrigues against him, Drakpa Gyaltsen decided to end his life.

He did so by pushing a ceremonial scarf down his own throat until he suffocated.

Before killing himself he called his best disciple. He informed him of the decision he had taken and ordered him to cremate his body after he died. He also foretold certain portents that would in fact come to pass during the cremation, proving the falseness of the accusations that had been made against him.

He said a dense column of black smoke would rise from his pyre. The smoke would take the form of an open hand.

During the cremation this did indeed happen. The disciple went down on his knees and implored the spirit of Drakpa Gyaltsen to remain on earth and revenge himself on his enemies.

Disaster struck the entire province of Central Tibet. Terrible epidemics killed men and animals. The Tibetan government suffered political and military defeats.

Even the Dalai Lama was not spared. His property was seriously damaged.

Then something particularly annoying happened. At midday each day, some malignant force would spill his plate of food on the ground.

It wasn't long before the astrologers and oracles discovered that a revengeful spirit was the cause of all these mishaps. They tried to placate it, but all their attempts were in vain.

The Tibetan government turned to the abbot of the Mindoling monastery. He was a very experienced lama. They asked him to capture the evil spirit and destroy it.

With his knowledge of magic, the lama managed to imprison the spirit in a ladle. But another malevolent spirit flew to the first one's rescue. The demon made the old lama lose his concentration and the imprisoned spirit slipped out of the ladle. All the lama's efforts to recapture it were in vain.

The Tibetan government and the spiritual leaders of the Gelug school decided to come to an agreement with the spirit. They offered to let him become the protector of the yellow-cap school. The spirit agreed and became the chief guardian of the Gelug monasteries under the name of Dorje Shugden.

René de Nebesky-Wojkowitz has written a significant book titled *Oracles and Demons of Tibet: The Cult and Iconography of the Tibetan Protective Deities*. The eighth chapter of the book is about Dorje Shugden.

René de Nebesky-Wojkowitz quotes a Tibetan text that listed the rituals to be carried out by followers of the Shugden cult. The text contains a detailed description of Dorje Shugden's appearance and celestial abode.

'Four gates lead into this four-cornered palace of skulls. The building is of a most frightening splendour. The four corners are made of red agate.

'The four gates consist of green emeralds. The four golden doorframes shine brilliantly. The door bolts are made of marvellous coral. The awnings consist of pearls, moistened with the blood of corpses.

'Inside, the pillars and beams are covered with human bones. Bowels form the hanging decorations. The projection of the roof is made of skeletons. The railing is a series of dried skulls.

'The roof is horrible to look at. It is built from the skeletons of the most ferocious Rakshasas.

'The parapet is a mass of bloody human hearts and heads. On it are "banners of victory" made of tiger and lion carcasses. Various demoniacal birds descend on them, scaring the enemies of religion with their screeching.

'On the roof there are the umbrellas of Tsongkhapa, protector of the religion, circular and yellow cloth flags. The points of all these are adorned with jewels and rivulets of blood drip from the edges of the cloth.

'Inside the palace, human corpses and horse carcasses are spread everywhere. The blood of man and horse streams together to form a lake. Human skins and tiger hides are stretched into curtains. The smoke from the human flesh burnt as offering spreads into every quarter of the world. Outside, on a platform, revived corpses and Rakshasas are jumping around as the skeletons perform their dance.

'There are "banners of victory" and circular banners made from the bodies of lions, tassels made of bleeding bowels, wreaths of various kinds of heads, ornaments made from the organs of the five senses, whisks made of human hair and other fearful things.

'Inside this gruesome supernatural abode, in the centre of a vehemently blazing firestorm, is the frightful Dorje Shugden.

'He has a dark red body and the savage expression of a fierce Rakshasa. His mouth is bottomless like the sky and his four teeth as sharp as the ice of a glacier. He rolls his tongue at lightning speed, causing the three worlds to quake.

'His forehead is contorted in terrible anger. His three bloodshot eyes stare full of hatred at the inimical Vighnas. The yellow-red flames from his eyebrows reduce the four classes of Bdud demons to ashes.

'His yellow-brown hair stands on end and in the centre above it, within a sun-mandala, resides the lord-protector and king of religion, the great Tsongkhapa, wearing a placid expression.

'By moving his ears rapidly, Dorje Shugden produces a fierce, evil-destroying wind that sweeps away evil-doers, oath-breakers and obstacle-creating demons. From his nostrils rain clouds come forth, bearing raging thunder and lightning that strike the land of the Vighnas.

'Dorje Shugden has one face and two hands. In his right hand he brandishes a flaming sword towards heaven.

'With this sword of meteoric iron, Dorje Shugden kills all malefactors and fiends.

'With his left hand he holds a skull cup to his chest. Within the cup are the organs of the five senses and warm blood.

'In the crook of his left arm is a mongoose capable of producing all the riches anyone could desire.'

René de Nebesky-Wojkowitz quotes other Tibetan texts in which Dorje Shugden is described in different ways.

In *Text Number 54*, for instance, Shugden is light-skinned, dresses like a 'minister' and straddles a purple snow lion.

This form was similar to the one in a sacred picture I bought in the Majnu ka Tilla bazaar in Delhi. In the colour picture, Shugden was wearing a round-brimmed hat. He wore the red and yellow clothing of a man of religion and straddled a blue and white snow lion. Both Shugden and the lion appeared to be smiling.

In a small shop in the Ladakh Bod Vihara in Delhi, I bought another picture of Shugden. In this one the protector of the Gelugpa looked angry and the lion he sat astride was gnashing its teeth.

These pictures were no longer sold in the Tibetan bazaars. It had become almost impossible to get one.

Unlike the Buddha and the bodhisattvas who were of Indian origin, Shugden belonged to another category of spirits and divinities. These 'protectors' were usually of Tibetan origin. They were local spirits going back to pre-Buddhist times. They were defeated in magic combat by the Indian masters, notably Guru Padmasambhava. Instead of being killed, these spirits were converted to Buddhism and agreed to become its protectors. Despite his more recent origins, Shugden too was a guardian spirit. His task was to defend the purity of the Gelug tradition (the yellow-cap school of monks) from the influence of the Nyigma (the red-cap school).

The terrible punishment of Dorje Shugden would be meted out to anyone who attempted to mix the teachings and rituals of the two traditions.

The Shugden cult spread within the high ranks of the powerful Gelug monasteries in Tibet and among Lhasa's conservative nobility.

After 1959 and the diaspora, the clergy and the nobles carried the Shugden cult into exile with them.

In India the cult spread rapidly to the lower rungs of the Tibetan community. For these Tibetans, Dorje Shugden was a divinity who could grant all wishes. He generally brought his followers luck and money.

In the beginning the Dalai Lama too performed propitiatory rites to Shugden. Then, all of a sudden, in 1976 he denounced the practice.

The Dalai Lama said that Shugden was neither a Buddha nor the incarnation of Drakpa Gyaltsen. He was a worldly deity or perhaps an evil spirit. His cult encouraged sectarianism in the Tibetan community in exile and hindered the cause of Tibetan independence.

Twenty years later, in 1996, the Dalai Lama condemned the Shugden cult even more explicitly. That year, on the occasion of the Tibetan New Year, he went to southern India for a Tantric initiation ceremony.

Before the ceremony the Dalai Lama invited all those present who refused to renounce the Shugden cult to leave the room.

'Tantric initiation implies a special relationship between the lama and the initiate,' the Dalai Lama said. 'If I were to initiate those who do not renounce Shugden, it would damage my health and shorten my life.'

The Tibetan government in exile immediately ranged itself alongside the Dalai Lama.

The *Resolution of the 6th June 1996* read: 'In the interest of Buddhism and the Tibetan national cause, His Holiness the

Dalai Lama has openly advised against the propitiation of Shugden. On behalf of the Tibetan people, both in and outside Tibet, the Assembly of Tibetan People's Deputies would like to express thanks and gratitude to His Holiness the Dalai Lama and make a pledge that we will abide by his every advice.

'...The departments, their branches and subsidiaries, monasteries and their branches that are functioning under the administrative control of the Tibetan Government in exile should be strictly instructed not to indulge in the propitiation of Shugden. We would like to clarify that if individual citizens propitiate Shugden it will harm the common interest of Tibet and the life of his Holiness the Dalai Lama and strengthen the spirits that are against the religion. This can be quite clearly and authentically established through texts and logic. Having said this, it is up to individuals themselves to decide as they like. We cannot force anyone to do anything against his or her wish. However, we would like to emphatically plead to the Shugden-worshippers that they stop taking Tantric initiations and teachings from His Holiness the Dalai Lama.'

The followers of Dorje Shugden reacted violently. The Tibetan government in exile began to receive threatening letters. The first was dated April 1996. It read, 'The Dalai Lama and the Tibetan donkey officials should resolve the problem truthfully or we will be forced to resort to bloodshed.'

On the 30th April the same year, the secretary of the department for religion and culture of the Tibetan government in exile and a representative of the Dalai Lama's office went to Mundgod in South India. They were to explain the Dalai Lama's position regarding the Shugden cult to the local Tibetan community. A packet was delivered to the two officials. It contained a knife. The message with it read: 'It wasn't possible for us to meet you this time. It'll have to be another time.'

The night of the 27th May 1996, someone made an attempt on the life of the venerable Thupten Wangyal, an ex-abbot of the Ganden monastery, in southern India. They burnt his house, but he managed to save himself. On the 9th January 1997 the hay loft of the granary of the Jangtse College in Mundgod was set on fire. The same month Geshe Thinley, a monk from Jangste College, was beaten up in the Majnu ka Tilla refugee camp in Delhi.

Geshe Kelsang Gyatso was among the monks who opposed the suppression of the Shugden cult most strongly.

Kelsang Gyatso was a monk from the Sera monastery in Tibet. Towards the end of the 1970s he moved to England. A Buddhist teacher, he published several books. In 1991 he founded a movement called 'New Kadampa Tradition' based in Ulverston. It quickly became one of the richest sects in Great Britain. Its followers venerated Kelsang Gyatso. They considered him a Buddha.

Like many Gelug monks, Kelsang Gyatso was a fervent Shugden devotee. He had taught his disciples to make this cult the focal point of their religious practice.

When the cult of Dorje Shugden was outlawed, Kelsang Gyatso's followers accused the Dalai Lama of intolerance and interference with their religious freedom. They made reference to the United Nations' declaration on human rights.

On the 23rd March 1996 the 'Dorje Shugden Devotees Charitable & Religious Society' was set up in Delhi. It had its headquarters in the Majnu ka Tilla refugee camp. Its members immediately mobilised in defence of the Shugden cult.

On the 5th May 1996 the Society wrote a letter to the twelfth Assembly of Tibetan People's Deputies. The letter read, 'As you are aware, the old government made a decision to ban the propitiation of Dorje Shugden. We know that a handful of poisonous and shameless officials persist in turning the milk sea of Tibet into a sea of boiling blood. We respectfully plead to the new Kashag and the Assembly to discuss the issue of Dorje Shugden fairly, according to the provisions of the democratic charter of Tibetans in exile, and to restore our human rights. We request you to send us a reply by the 14th of this month; and there should be no procrastination. We, in our present state of desperation, have made up our minds to resort to desperate measures if such a decision is not made.'

On the 17th June 1996 Jampel Yeshe, president of the Dorje Shugden Devotees Charitable & Religious Society, wrote a letter to Deve Gowda, then Prime Minister of India: 'We are seeking to draw your attention to a problem that requires an urgent solution. We have become aware of serious human rights violations against many thousands of our members living in India. These human rights violations are being carried out by the Tibetan government in exile headed by the Dalai Lama against tens of thousands of Tibetans who are living in India and who worship one particular Buddhist Deity known as Dorje Shugden. This Deity has been worshipped for many generations by millions of people throughout the Mahayana Buddhist world.'

The letter contained strong accusations against the Tibetan government in exile. It was accused in particular of:

1. Having forced thousands of Tibetans to sign a declaration renouncing the Dorje Shugden cult.
2. Having threatened to cut off foreign aid funds to groups of Tibetan refugees who refused to sign the declaration.
3. Having supported Tibetan Women's Association squads and Tibetan Youth Congress militants in their actions against worshippers of Shugden.
4. More specifically, these squads appeared to have stormed the houses of Shugden devotees, destroyed pictures of Shugden and treated his devotees badly.

5. Having expelled the children of Shugden devotees from Tibetan schools and sacked government employees who had not renounced their cult.

The letter ended with an urgent request to the Indian prime minister to 'put an immediate end to the persecution of the worshippers of Dorje Shugden in India.'

***

It was when the tension between the Tibetan government in exile and the Dorje Shugden Devotees Charitable & Religious Society was at its peak that I decided to pay a visit to the Society's headquarters.

None of my friends in the Tibetan Youth Congress in Delhi wanted to come with me.

'It's dangerous,' they told me.

I reached the Majnu ka Tilla refugee camp at two in the afternoon.

Parallel to the Main Road, another road ran through the New Camp and the Old Camp.

Many of the shops were shut for the afternoon siesta.

I decided to have lunch at the 'Tee Dee Restaurant'.

The restaurant was on the first floor of a building facing the headquarters of the Tibetan Welfare Office. It was summer and the ceiling fans in the restaurants were whirring at full speed. I ordered 'tingmo' (lightly baked bread) and 'pingsha' (a kind of stew).

When the waiter brought my food, I asked him if he knew where the Dorje Shugden Society headquarters were.

The young Tibetan looked at me in surprise. 'I don't know,' he said. He seemed anxious to back away from my table.

As I was eating, a monk approached me. He had been sitting by himself at a table near mine. 'I heard you asking about the Dorje Shugden Society,' he said in a low voice. 'I live in their hostel. If you wish, I can take you there.'

The outside of the building in which the Society was located was made of red granite. There were the 'banners of victory' — large cylinders covered in copperplate — on the roof.

I climbed the steps to the entrance.

The lobby was dark and dirty. It contained stacks of old beds, chairs with missing bottoms and two rusting refrigerators. Someone was on the telephone at the reception. Two Tibetans were playing carrom on a wooden board that was slippery with talcum powder. A group of youngsters looked at me curiously.

I waited for the telephone call to end.

I asked the man at the reception if I could speak to the secretary of the Society. He told me the secretary's office was elsewhere and that someone would take me there.

The office of the Dorje Shugden Society was in a lane in the Old Camp at a right angle to the Main Road. There was a coloured flag on the door — a vertical ochre band on the left, then five horizontal stripes in blue, yellow, green, white and red with the wheel of Dharma overprinted on them.

The person who had accompanied me rang the bell several times.

A few minutes later a Tibetan who looked about thirty opened the door. He wore a pair of jeans and was buttoning a check shirt. A young woman slipped across a dark corridor behind him.

The man in jeans smiled at me. He spoke with a slight American twang. His name was N.K. Tenzin. He was the 'Secretary' of the Society. He was a monk, he informed me, jeans and check shirt notwithstanding. He led me to the first floor.

N.K. Tenzin's office was small. It had a large desk. There was a colour photo of the tenth Panchen Lama in a gold frame on one wall.

On the desk was a black and white photograph of Mahatma Gandhi.

The young woman reappeared, carrying a red plastic thermos of hot tea.

'Who is this Shugden, exactly?' I asked the 'Secretary'.

The man rose and went into the room next door. He returned with some photocopies and a book.

'You can keep the photocopies,' he said.

They were the writings of Geshe Kelsang Gyatso, downloaded from the website of the New Kadampa Tradition in Cumbria in Great Britain.

'To guide human beings,' wrote Geshe Kelsang, 'Dorje Shugden appears in different forms. Sometimes he takes on a pacific form. Sometimes an angry one. Sometimes he appears as an ordinary person, sometimes as a bodhisattva. Or he might appear as a Hinayana Buddhist, or a non-Buddhist, or even in a non-human form. There are many emanations of the Buddha. And so it is difficult to establish with any certainty who is one of these emanations and who is not.'

The book N.K. Tenzin showed me was titled *The Worship of the Guru*. It was in three languages — English, Tibetan and Chinese. It had been published in China.

The 'Secretary' gave me an audiocassette with the 'Prayer of Protection' addressed to the 'Diamond King' (Dorje Shugden). The cassette too was made in China.

N.K. Tenzin spoke persuasively. He said, 'All Tibetans respect the Dalai Lama, but...' and began his attack.

'Those who win the Nobel Peace Prize have always suffered,' he said. 'Often they have spent long years in jail. He (the Dalai Lama) won it without so much as a scratch on him. He says he is a spiritual leader, and then we find him advertising Apple computers in magazines.' The 'Secretary' showed me a glossy American magazine. There was a black and white photograph of the Dalai Lama. 'Think different,' the slogan read. On the bottom of the page, on the right hand side, was the company's multicoloured apple logo.

I asked the 'Secretary' to tell me about the Shugden cult.

'An immense majority of Tibetans venerate Shugden,' he told me. 'The Dalai Lama has caused a lot of sorrow in the Tibetan community in and outside Tibet with the position he has taken. We are persecuted. Discriminated against. They ask us to sign a declaration renouncing the Shugden cult. If we don't do it we lose our jobs as government employees and they don't issue the document we need to travel abroad.'

The 'Secretary' of the Dorje Shugden Devotees Charitable & Religious Society stopped to take breath. He added, 'The Dalai Lama says he wants freedom for Tibet. To obtain it he says he follows "the Middle Way". Tibetans living abroad don't give a damn. They work, they trade...We'll never get anything this way. If we really want things to change we have to go back to Tibet. We can't fight if everyone stays abroad doing their own thing.'

The 'Secretary' offered me another cup of tea and continued: 'The image the world is given, of a Tibetan community united around the Dalai Lama, is false. There's more than just Shugden. There are two Panchen Rinpoches. There are two Karmapas. The Tibetan community is divided...'

The Chinese didn't slip let the opportunity. They immediately sought to turn the division within the Tibetan community in exile to their advantage.

China's Tibet magazine published a long article titled 'Dalai Disavows Guardian of Buddhist Doctrine' in its Issue 6, 1996.

The article read: 'Gyaigen Xudian (Gyalchen Shugden), or Doje Xudian (Dorje Shugden) which means Diamond

Guardian Spirit, is the famous guardian of doctrine of the Gelug sect of Tibetan Buddhism.

'The Dalai and his followers have repeatedly declared that Gyaigen Xudian is a "Han Ghost" who lacks favour with Negun (Nechung), the main guardian of Buddhist doctrine. In March 1966 the Dalai Lama issued a ridiculous accusation that the guardian of Tibetan Buddhism was in some way affecting his government in exile...

'...The Dalai stressed that anyone worshipping the guardian would be acting against the "common cause of Tibet" and would quite simply be yearning for his own early demise. The Dalai's cronies rushed to areas in India and Nepal inhabited by Tibetans. They forced Tibetans to obey the Dalai's order to abandon the worship of Gyaigen Xudian, a figure worshipped by generations of their families. The Dalai's men proceeded to visit monasteries and private houses destroying statues of the guardian of Buddhist doctrine.

'The Dalai has been leading a life in exile for the past thirty-seven years. He has yearned for the day the Communist Party of China would step down. He predicted that the 1990s would be a period ripe for Tibet to "win independence" and that the "Chinese Communist regime" would be toppled between 1995 and 1996. He travelled far and wide seeking support for the independence of Tibet, with his efforts supported by funds raised from Tibetans residing overseas. The group providing his funds, however, is becoming increasingly disappointed to see that the Dalai Lama has been reduced to a mouthpiece of international anti-China forces, and that his predictions are sheer nonsense.

'China is in fact gaining ever-greater international prestige, and Tibetans are leading a better life. Tibetan compatriots residing abroad express amazement at the freedom of religious belief enjoyed by their counterparts. Discontent with the Dalai

Lama continues to grow and people have lost confidence in the call for "Tibetan independence".'

Many followers of the Shugden cult in the West went to China and obtained aid. In India, monks who applied for visas at the Chinese embassy were asked, 'Are you Shugden worshippers?' They only had to reply 'Yes' to be given a visa.

The Chinese government set up a 'Shugden Foundation' in Lhasa. Ten thousand yuan were allocated for the restoration of the Dorje Shugden temple in the Panglung area of Lhasa.

Beijing sought to divide the Tibetan community in exile in order to weaken the struggle for independence.

For the Dalai Lama, the banning of the Shugden cult had a diametrically opposite meaning. Shugden was a partisan spirit. He was the protector of only the Gelug tradition. He was opposed to the other three schools of Buddhism - Nyingma, Sakya and Kagyu. He was even hostile to the Bon. Although he belonged to the Gelug school, the Dalai Lama offered himself as a guide for all Tibetan Buddhists. He wanted his people to be united. He was trying to create a 'national' culture to counteract the Chinese one, which was trying, on the other hand, to destroy it.

On the 30th September 1997 the Dalai Lama spoke to the members of the Gu-Chu-Sum association in McLeod Ganj. He tackled the Dorje Shugden problem once again. He said, 'As regards Dolgyal (Shugden), we must be very careful. I have decided to ban this practice in the light of the controversies it has caused for over three hundred years, since the time of the fifth Dalai Lama. My decision was not motivated by other factors. It is as if we have an illness to deal with and surgery has to be undergone. In the beginning there can be some negative reactions. That is natural. But it doesn't worry me too much.

Now there are those who say I want to destroy the Gelug teachings. Let them say it. I am trying to act for the good of all Tibetans. It doesn't interest me what these critics say. The Buddha too was criticised when he was alive. The same thing happened with Tsongkhapa. I am an ordinary human being. It's natural that people should criticise me. There's nothing to be surprised about. But it is important not to be deceived by these people. When I tell you to watch out I am not asking you to clash with them, not even when they kill, set fire to houses and try to burn people alive.

'The investigations carried out by the Indian police make it clear who murdered Geshe Lobsang Gyatso. It was six monks from Sera Me and Ganden Shartse in the south of India. They were all people who had recently arrived from Tibet. Their original intention was probably to study in our monasteries. But then someone convinced them to commit this terrible crime, either with money or through indoctrination.

'Now all six monks have fled back to Tibet. This is what I have been told. But we must limit ourselves to informing people and keeping them alert. We must not, for any reason, resort to violence towards the followers of Shugden.'

* * *

The Tibetan community in exile was very disturbed by the murder of Lobsang Gyatso.

Two letters were added to the evidence in the investigation into the triple murder.

The first was dated 3rd July 1996 and bore the stamp of the Dorje Shugden Charitable & Religious Society in Delhi. It was addressed 'To the morally degenerate Lobsang Gyatso, who is a disgrace to the Institute of Buddhist Dialectics.' The letter read: 'We came to Dharamsala three times. In which nunnery were you hiding then? Instead of writing warped compositions, you should come down to Delhi with courage and meet us like the louse meets a thumbnail. However, if your guilty conscience does not afford you the courage to come down, we will come to you...'

After the murder, another letter was sent to the Assembly of Tibetan People's Deputies. The letter, hand-written in Tibetan, was dated the 31st March 1997. The text read: 'Alas! Divisionist Da (the Dalai Lama) and Sam (Samdhong Rinpoche, Speaker of the Assembly of Tibetan People's Deputies). You have accumulated everlasting bad karma by creating rifts in the monastic community and thus setting in motion a cycle of bloodshed. You pretend to be the followers of the Buddha. But look at your brand of non-violent peaceful path. In the *Great Arya Liberation Sutra* it is stated, "Creating a breach among the monks is akin to killing all the human beings and other sentient beings in the Three Realms. And it brings as much bad karmic results."

'Therefore, you two, Da and Sam, are not the followers of the Buddha. The Lord Buddha forsook his kingdom, although he was born a king, whereas you two are only after political power.

'Did you enjoy eating the three carcasses at the time of the Happy Fire-Ox Losar this year? You will be treated to many more carcasses if you continue the present practice. Signed, Monk Lobsang Jungney from Sera Monastery in South India.'

The first article on the investigation was published in *The Indian Express* on the 25th February 1997. The short article quoted Kangra police commissioner Rajeev Kumar Singh. 'There is a new development,' he said, 'but I cannot reveal the details because it could compromise the investigation.'

Two other articles published in the Hindi daily *Jansatta* of the 28th April 1997 and the Chandigarh-based *The Tribune* on the 29th November 1997 respectively laid out all the details of the triple homicide.

The first article was titled 'Dharamsala murder work of pro-Shugden groups.' The second was titled 'Another two pro-Shugden activists identified as the killers.'

The sources quoted were police commissioner Rajeev Kumar Singh as before and deputy inspector I.D. Bhandari.

This is how the Indian police pieced the facts together.

On the evening of the 31st January 1997 an aircraft with Lobsang Gyatso on board landed at New Delhi's Indira Gandhi International Airport. The director of the Institute of Buddhist Dialectics had returned from Hong Kong, where he had held a series of conferences. Lobsang Gyatso left immediately for McLeod Ganj by car. Six young Tibetans followed him in a taxi with the licence plate number THA 4283. The youths told the taxi driver, a certain Mangal Ram, that some of their baggage had remained in the car in front of them by mistake.

In Ambala the taxi broke down, interrupting the youths' chase. One of them called Delhi from a telephone booth. The number he dialled was that of the Dorje Shugden Society in Majnu ka Tilla.

From Ambala the six Tibetans took another taxi to Kangra. Here they spent the night of the 1st February at the Grand Hotel. The hotel staff later recognised the cloth bag that Lobsang Gyatso had managed to snatch from his assailants before he died. The bag contained a pair of gloves, an electric torch, a knife and photocopied leaflets defending the Shugden cult.

The leaflets threatened 'bloodshed'.

The Kangra Hotel employees also recognised two of the six murderers in photographs.

They were twenty-two-year-old Tenzin Choezin from the

Sera monastery at Bylakuppe and Lobsang Choejam, twenty-five, from the Ganden Shartse monastery in Mundgod. Both were natives of the Chathreng province of Tibet.

Tenzin Choezin had been expelled from the Sera monastery because of his violent opposition to critics of the Shugden cult. Despite his expulsion, he continued to live in the monastery.

Some months later the police identified another two Tibetans who were part of the group, Thupten Choden and Lobsang Phuntosk.

On the evening of the 4th February, the six youths reached McLeod Ganj in a taxi from Kangra. They got down at Dolma Chowk. It was six in the evening and it was already dark.

The youths took the descending road that led to Main Temple. They walked fast, huddling together. One of them was wearing a black baseball cap. He had a khaki coloured cloth bag slung over one shoulder.

The small green gate of the Institute of Buddhist Dialectics was ajar. The six youths entered. They climbed the stairs almost at a run. They knocked on the door of the director of the Institute.

'Geshe-la,' said the youth wearing the black baseball cap.

Thupten Ngodup

On Monday 27th April 1998 in New Delhi it was already summer. The temperature was well above forty degrees.

A hot wind scattered the yellow sand of the Rajasthan desert over the city.

The birds were sitting under the trees, their mouths wide open, seeking a little shade.

Doctors advised people to drink a lot of water and cover their heads.

The newspapers talked of fires. One unextinguished match would be enough to send an entire shantytown up in flames.

That Monday marked the start of an official visit to India by General Fu Quanyou, Army Chief of Staff of the People's Republic of China.

For the Indians, it was an important visit. There had been a lapse that had to be remedied. Some months earlier the Indian defence minister George Fernandes had said, 'China is our main enemy.' Beijing had registered an official protest.

During his visit General Fu Quanyou would meet the Prime Minister Atal Behari Vajpayee, the Indian Army Chief of Staff General V.P. Malik and the selfsame Defence Minister George Fernandes.

The Indians had several grievances. First of all there was the problem of redefining the so-called Line of Actual Control (LAC). On many Chinese maps, Sikkim and most of Arunachal Pradesh were indicated as belonging to the People's Republic of China. Then there was the problem of the M-11 and M-9 missiles that China continued to supply to Pakistan. Finally, there was the problem of the heliport the Chinese had constructed in the north-eastern frontier area. The Chinese said the heliport was in the Sumdarongchu valley, on their side of the line of control. The Indians said it had been built on their territory.

The Chinese did not consider India a real military threat. Any comparison between the two armies was clearly in their favour. There was just one irritant to be eliminated — the Tibetans' separatist activities on Indian territory.

This had been openly expressed in diplomatic language. General Fu Quanyou was in fact accompanied by Lieutenant-General Liao Xilong, commander of the military region of Chengdu, which included Tibet.

The Chinese were only repeating an existing concept. In December 1996, during Chinese President Jiang Zemin's state visit to India, he had been accompanied by Gyalsten Norbu, Governor of the Autonomous Region of Tibet.

The Indian diplomats had got the message.

In New Delhi a hunger strike unto death had been going on for 48 days in the central Sansad Marg, right in front of Jantar Mantar, the astronomical observatory built by Maharaja Jai Singh II in 1725.

The strikers were six Tibetans.

Two hundred Indian policemen moved in to stop the protest on the night between the 26th and 27th April. Three of the six Tibetans were forced into police vans and taken to hospital.

On the morning of the 27th April, a few hours before the visit of General Fu Quanyou to Delhi, a contingent of five hundred Indian paramilitary troops had also stopped the protest of the three remaining demonstrators.

But there had been a mishap. A Tibetan had tried to commit suicide. He had covered himself with petrol and set himself on fire.

The six Tibetans' hunger strike had begun on Tuesday 10th March 1998. It had been organised by the Tibetan Youth Congress (TYC), the most important political movement to emerge from among the Tibetan refugees in India.

Squeezed between Sansad Marg (Parliament Street) and Jantar Mantar in New Delhi was a small, trapezoid-shaped park with a high, green-painted iron fence.

To the right of the small park was a public toilet made of white tiles with 'Public Conveniences' written over it.

Many of the protest demonstrations held in the Indian capital took place in this little park. Almost every day there were meetings, sit-ins, banners, slogans, angry fists and excited people there.

The TYC militants had set up a big tent on the grass, among the neem trees. Long bamboo poles held up a sackcloth cover.

That 10th March there had been the usual demonstration in all the Tibetan centres in India in memory of the 1959 Lhasa insurrection.

In Delhi, Tibetan boys and girls wearing school uniform had paraded at the head of a long procession. They wore white shirts and ties. They had black headbands around their foreheads with the words FREE TIBET written on them in white. At the head of the procession was a large banner: 'Tibet for the Tibetans.'

The entire population of the Majnu ka Tilla and Ladakh Bod Vihara refugee camps followed the banner.

The police managed to keep the demonstrators away from the Chinese embassy. The procession then headed towards Parliament Street.

The preceding night at midnight, the 'hunger strike unto death' of the six Tibetans, one for every million inhabitants of the Land of Snows, had begun under the Tibetan Youth Congress tent.

When I went to Delhi's Jantar Mantar the six Tibetans were already on the twenty-seventh day of their strike.

Traffic on Parliament Street went past rapidly, seemingly indifferent to the protest of the Tibetans.

In the park in front of the astronomical observatory there were coloured banners everywhere.

One red banner bore the words 'Hunger strike unto death.' It was signed 'Tibetan Youth Congress.' There was a blue banner: 'UN, we want justice.' It was signed 'Alumni Association Kathmandu.' There was a white banner: 'UN: reopen the debate on Tibet.' It was signed 'R.T.Y.C. Kathmandu.'

There was a colour painting of a Chinese People's Liberation Army soldier on a big white sheet. He wore a green uniform and cap with a visor and the red star. He had his machine gun trained on a young Tibetan woman.

The woman was wearing a chuba and a pagden, the apron with coloured stripes. In her right hand the woman carried the flag of independent Tibet. With her left, she held a babe in arms close. The caption read, 'Ruthless Suppression of Tibetan Women and Children by the Red Chinese.'

A hand-written poster listed the Tibetan Youth Congress' requests to the United Nations:

'We request:
1. The reopening of the debate on the Tibetan question, starting from the 1959, 1961 and 1965 UN resolutions.
2. The setting-up of an enquiry commission to verify respect for human rights in Chinese-occupied Tibet.
3. The nomination of a UN special envoy to facilitate a peaceful solution to the Tibetan question and start the procedure for a referendum through which the Tibetan people can freely express their wishes.'

A double-sided board was propped on the grass. It said, in English and Hindi: 'Tibetan Youth Congress. Fast unto

Death. 27th day. Started on 10th March 1998.'

The number of days the strike had gone on was written in chalk on a rectangular black space. The number was changed every day.

The six Tibetans lay under the tarpaulin on rope beds covered with thin mattresses.

Their clothes were hung out to dry on cords behind them. There were threadbare rugs on the ground and cardboard boxes of Bisleri mineral water under the beds.

The strikers had sunken cheeks and a dull-eyed gaze.

The shadow of death had begun to be reflected in their eyes.

The strikers were five men and one woman.

DAWA TSERING was 53 and had a wife and six children. He was born in Khatak in the district of Lhoka in Central Tibet.

In 1960 he ran away from Tibet and found refuge in India. In 1962 he enlisted in the Indian army. In 1972 he left the army and began working at the office of the Tibetan Freedom Movement in the Kunpheling refugee camp in Sikkim.

He said, 'I'm not afraid to die. If I were to die a natural death I'd leave my wife and kids anyway. If I die during this hunger strike at least I'll have managed to draw the world's attention to the Tibetan question.

'In Tibet, Tibetans cannot even meet to discuss their problems. If we don't do it, who will take care of them?'

DAWA GYALPO was 50. He was born in Nagari in western Tibet. In 1960, when he was twelve, he escaped to India. Like many others, he crossed the Himalaya range on foot. In 1971 he worked for a while at the Library of Tibetan Works and Archives in Dharamsala.

He had been a member of the Tibetan Youth Congress

since its formation.

He went to Mustang, in one of the teams of Tibetan guerrillas who committed sabotage against the Chinese. When the movement broke up he found work as a tourist guide. In 1985 he managed a brief visit to Tibet.

He said, 'In the Jokhang in Lhasa, in front of the statue of Jowo Shakyamuni, I made a vow to dedicate the rest of my life to the liberation of Tibet.

'As Tibetans we must admit that we are defeated until such time as we manage to get the Dalai Lama back to the Potala palace in a Tibet that is finally free.

'If I die during this hunger strike, my death will have been a small step ahead towards this goal.'

KUSANG was 70. He was born in Shelkar in central Tibet. His parents were nomads. He ran away from Tibet in 1976. For eight years he worked on a road construction site in Gangtok, Sikkim. In 1986 he moved to the refugee camp of Puruwala in North India. Here he began fighting for Tibetan independence.

After almost a month of hunger striking he said, 'The UN continues to be indifferent to our requests. Death is just around the corner for us now.'

KARMA SICHOE was 25 years old. He was the youngest of the group. He had spent his childhood at the Tibetan Children's Village in Dharamsala. His mother died when he was still a child. His papers said 'Father unknown'.

He dropped out after eight years of school. He began working in a thangka painters' studio. He became very good at it. Six years later he moved to Nepal where he started up a 'Thangka Painting Association'.

During the hunger strike people said to him, 'You're still so young. Why have you decided to risk your life?' He replied,

'I prefer to die young fighting than live to old age as a refugee.'

PALZOM was the only woman in the group. She was 68. She was born in Shigatse in Tibet. At the beginning of the 1960s the Chinese had killed her father. During the Cultural Revolution the Red Guards accused her mother of having hidden weapons for some monks. Palzom's mother too died during a 'thamzing', a struggle session.

On the 1st October 1987 Palzom was in the Barkor in Lhasa throwing stones at Chinese policemen and soldiers. Afterwards she managed to flee to India, where she took part in two peace marches for Tibet's freedom.

She said, 'I'm not afraid to die. I already died many times when the Chinese humiliated my parents and me in Tibet. I'm not looking for revenge now. I only want justice.'

YUNDRUNG TSERING was 28. He was a childhood friend of Karma Sichoe, the youngest of the group. Both of them lived in McLeod Ganj. They had both gone to the Tibetan Children's Village school and learned to paint thangkas together.

He said, 'At the beginning of the hunger strike I had terrible stomach cramps, for days. Now I don't wish to eat anymore. Freedom for Tibet - that's my only remaining wish.'

A second group of militants was already ready to replace the six Tibetans once their 'hunger strike unto death' had come to its extreme end.

The six substitutes were Jampa Kalsang, 23; Tsering Dorje, 37; Thupten Ngodup, 60; Kalden Norbu, 47; Tsering Gonkyab, 55 and Phuntsok Semsang, 25.

The Tibetan Youth Congress kept a diary of the strike.

10th March 1998. The 'hunger strike unto death' began at midnight on the night between the 9th and 10th March to recall the UN's attention to the Tibetan question. Under the Jantar

Mantar tent Tseten Norbu, president of the Tibetan Youth Congress, offered the six strikers a khata, a white silk scarf. It marked the start of the protest.

23rd March. Richard Gere visited the six striking Tibetans. Later, at a press conference in Delhi, the American actor said, 'India is the land where Buddhism was born. India and Tibet have always had a special relationship. Today, India must face the Tibetan question more courageously.'

25th March. An 'All India Students for Tibet' delegation visited the five men and the woman on a hunger strike. The students drew up a motion of solidarity.

2nd April. The Dalai Lama went to the Jantar Mantar in Delhi to visit the six Tibetans on a hunger strike. After the meeting the Dalai Lama said, "I told the strikers that I admire their determination and courage. But I also reminded them that I consider a hunger strike unto death to be an act of violence.

'I am against any form of violence, against others and oneself. Unfortunately, this time I am unable to suggest another form of struggle. I can only say that having seen these six Tibetans on a hunger strike unto death has been like seeing Tibetan civilisation die in front of me.'

3rd April. The Lithuanian parliament's 'Group for Relations with Tibet' wrote a letter to the UN Secretary General and the UN Human Rights Commission: 'Six precious human lives will be shattered if the UN continues to ignore the requests of the strikers.'

7th April. The Australian Senate approved a motion expressing 'preoccupation about and empathy with' the six Tibetans on a hunger strike.

9th April. Mary Robinson, UN High Commissioner for Human Rights, said she was ready to go to Tibet to personally verify the human rights situation in the country.

10th April. Wei Jinsheng, the Chinese militant fighting for democracy and human rights in the People's Republic of China, expressed his preoccupation about 'the state of my Tibetan friends who are on a hunger strike.' Wei Jinsheng asked the UN and the international community to 'permit my Tibetan friends not to die and to carry forward their peaceful and non-violent struggle.'

12th April. Adam Dieng, General Secretary of the International Jurists Commission, visited the six strikers in Delhi. He said, 'The International Jurists Commission has nothing against China, but fights for justice. The Tibetan people are fighting for a just cause that we too support.'

14th April. The students of Delhi University, Jawaharlal Nehru University and Jamia Millia Islamia went on a twenty-four-hour hunger strike to express their solidarity with the six striking Tibetans.

15th April. Kofi Annan, Secretary-General of the UN, called upon the six Tibetans to suspend their strike 'for humanitarian reasons.'

21st April. In a message to the Tibetan Youth Congress, the Norwegian government expressed its concern for the state of the strikers and emphasised that it wanted to 'continue broaching the Tibetan question in all the international forums.'

The Tibetan Youth Congress received a letter of solidarity from the underground 'Tibet Freedom' movement operating inside Tibet. The letter, dated 16th April, said, 'Tibetans in Tibet admire the heroism, courage and dedication of the six striking Tibetans.'

24th April. In a release, the European Union presidency appealed to the six strikers to stop their protest.

26th April. Two hundred Indian policemen burst into the Jantar Mantar in Delhi at midnight and removed three of the six strikers. Dawa Gyalpo, Dawa Tsering and Karma Sichoe were taken to Ram Manohar Lohia Hospital.

27th April. It was the first day of the official visit to India by the Chinese general Fu Quanyou. At six in the morning a contingent of five hundred Indian paramilitary soldiers forcibly stopped the hunger strike of the remaining three Tibetans. Yundrung Tsering, Kusang and Palzom were also taken to Delhi's Ram Manohar Lohia Hospital.

Thupten Ngodup, one of the six Tibetans in the second 'batch', sprinkled petrol over himself in the public toilet and set himself alight to protest the police operation. He was rushed to hospital with ninety-degree burns all over his body.

28th April. The Dalai Lama visited Thupten Ngodup and the other six strikers in the Ram Manohar Hospital in Delhi.

At 00.15 hours on the 29th April, Thupten Ngodup died.

Chayang Tharchin of the Department of Information and International Relations of the Tibetan government in exile filmed the self-immolation scene.

It was an extraordinary record.

The footage showed the policemen in berets and khaki uniforms surrounding the strikers' tent.

A Tibetan in pyjama bottoms and a purple T-shirt wriggled out of the police cordon.

The next frame showed a corner of the public toilet, a big neem tree and, in the middle, a mushroom-shaped fire.

The silhouette of a man could be seen in the flames. He was jumping and waving his arms.

People ran away, frightened. They were shouting.

The man in the ball of fire could be seen moving towards the tent of the Tibetan Youth Congress. Above him, hung on the branches of the trees, was a banner with 'U.N.O. We want justice' on it.

The man wrapped in flames raised his folded hands above

his head.

The Tibetan women present could be heard screaming. The video panned to the policemen and the militants of the Tibetan Youth Congress trying to put out the fire with blankets. The screams continued in the background.

The man fell to the ground, still wrapped in flames.

The film stopped abruptly.

The man in the flames was Thupten Ngodup, a sixty-year-old Tibetan.

He was one of the six Tibetan Youth Congress militants who was supposed to replace the first lot of strikers once their protest had reached its tragic end.

Witnesses would later say that when Thupten Ngodup had been seized by the flames he had shouted 'Bod gyalo,' 'Tibet will win,' and 'Bod rangzen,' 'Free Tibet,' in a strangled voice. Then, hands folded above his head, in a faint voice he had whispered 'Long live His Holiness the Dalai Lama.'

The police put the man in an ambulance.

With sirens at full blast they carried him to the Ram Manohar Lohia Hospital, where doctors found ninety-degree burns all over his body. 'His condition is critical,' they said. 'His chances of survival are minimal.'

In the late afternoon of the 28th April the Dalai Lama went to the Lohia Hospital in Delhi to visit Thupten Ngodup and the six Tibetans who had been forced to stop their hunger strike.

When the Dalai Lama entered Thupten Ngodup tried to sit up.

He brought his bandaged hands together respectfully.

The Dalai Lama asked Thupten Ngodup if he could hear him.

With a movement of his head Thupten replied yes.

'You must not feel hatred for the Chinese,' the Dalai Lama told him. 'It is contrary to the principles of Buddhism to hate people. Your action was important. You made people aware of our cause in a way that they have never been before now. Even if you do not manage to survive, all Tibetans shall remember you with respect forever. I shall pray for your new life to commence at the earliest.'

Hours later, well into the night, Thupten Ngodup asked for a sweet to suck on. A few minutes later, he asked for it to be removed from his mouth. He also asked for a sip of water.

Fifteen minutes after midnight, Thupten Ngodup died.

Four days before he burnt himself alive, Thupten Ngodup had given an interview to the Norwegian station of 'Voice of Tibet' radio.

'What is your name?'

'Thupten Ngodup.'

'How old are you?'

'Sixty.'

'You are in the second batch of participants in the hunger strike. What made you take this decision?'

'I decided to take part in the hunger strike simply because I am a Tibetan. And, as a Tibetan, I have a duty to accomplish.'

'Do you have family in India?'

'No. All my relatives live in Tibet.'

'Where do you live?'

'Near the Tsechokling monastery in McLeod Ganj. I'm a cook.'

'Yours is a "hunger strike unto death". Aren't you frightened?'

'No. There is no fear in my heart. When I met the six strikers for the first time, I was very happy. It has been almost forty years since we lost our homeland. Our culture and religion have been thrown out like rubbish. Today there are many people all over the world who support our cause. Gyalwa Rinpoche (the Dalai Lama) has tried to carry on his programme through a peaceful "middle way". He has also tried to dialogue with the Chinese. But there have been no results. This is why the situation has become desperate today. The six people who replied to the appeal of the Tibetan Youth Congress wanted to react to this situation. They are not afraid to die. And when it will be my turn, I too will face death fearlessly.'

'How do you intend to carry out your protest?'

'As I said, the Tibet situation is desperate. My hunger strike will be even more drastic than that of my six companions. I will refuse even water and I won't allow my body to be massaged.'

'Do you have anything to say to Tibetans living in Tibet?'

'I am sure that Tibetans living in Tibet will not only continue their struggle but that they will intensify it. I want to say just one thing to all Tibetans - no one is going to give us freedom. We will have to get it by ourselves.'

At dawn on the 29th April Thupten Ngodup's body was taken to Lady Hardinge Medical College to be autopsied. A cortege of twelve cars then escorted the bier, wrapped in a Tibetan flag, to the Majnu ka Tilla refugee camp in Delhi's northern suburbs.

The bier was placed in front of the refugee camp's small Gelug monastery.

All the Tibetans in the Indian capital were there to bid Thupten Ngodup a final farewell. People were in tears. 'He was a hero,' a weeping, middle-aged Tibetan told me. 'Only very few of us would have had the courage to do what he did for our cause.'

That day all the Tibetan schools, offices and shops all over

India remained closed.

On Thursday 30th the bier containing the mortal remains of Thupten Ngodup was transported to McLeod Ganj in an air-conditioned minivan.

When it reached the small Himalayan town the coffin was placed in an open jeep and taken to Tsuglagkhang, the Central Cathedral.

There were three flags on the emerald-green jeep — two Tibetan flags and the yellow flag of the Tibetan Youth Congress.

Hundreds of Tibetans were lined up along Temple Road.

Thrown from the roadside, the khatas - white silk scarves - fell on the jeep like shooting stars.

Three Tibetan Youth Congress members heaped the scarves on top of the coffin.

As the vehicle passed hundreds of closed fists were raised to the sky. 'U.N.O. we want freedom,' shouted the Tibetans of McLeod Ganj.

The coffin was put on a raised platform right in front of Tsuglagkhang.

A cloth banner hung on the platform railing. On it was written:

> *We Salute and Pay our Homage*
> *To Mr. Thupten Ngodup for Sacrificing*
> *His Life for the Cause of Tibet.*

There were two large colour photographs above the banner.

The photo on the left was a close-up of Thupten Ngodup's face, his forehead furrowed with lines and a melancholy smile on his lips.

In the photo on the right Thupten Ngodup was a dark silhouette surrounded by flames. It was an enlarged still from the video shot at the Jantar Mantar in Delhi.

The square in front of the Tsuglagkhang was heaving with people.

The official speakers took turns on the veranda of the Central Cathedral.

Tseten Norbu, President of the Tibetan Youth Congress, said: 'With his martyrdom, Thupten Ngodup has brought back dignity to our lives. He has shown the world that although Tibetans are not permitted to live honourably, they know how to die with dignity. With his sacrifice Thupten Ngodup wanted to cry out the desperation of six million Tibetans for the world to hear.'

The McLeod Ganj cremation grounds were nearly three kilometres from the town centre. One crossed a stretch of the Main Road that led to Dharamsala, then took a narrow tar road that snaked through woods of pine and rhododendron. The sunlight filtered through the trees as it would through the windows of a cathedral.

There was a metal structure with a sloping gable roof. Six short iron beams pushed through the ash in the clearing in front of the structure. They served to hold the pyre still. A brook gurgled among some large rocks at a short distance. Everything was silent and peaceful. The sound of the water and the twittering of birds were all that was to be heard.

Eight bearers in dark chubas hefted the coffin covered with a Tibetan flag onto their shoulders. A long procession began to move slowly. Three Indian policemen in khaki uniforms carrying bamboo canes led it. Behind them came a monk holding up a big thangka painting like a flag. Tseten Norbu, president of the TYC, in a grey chuba, followed him. Immediately after that was the coffin.

Then came the citizens of McLeod Ganj - thousands of people, many of them with tears in their eyes.

Step by step the procession travelled the three kilometres between Tsuglagkhang and the cremation grounds.

The woodpile was ready. The coffin was placed on the ground. The bearers removed the Tibetan flag.

'Pawo Thupten Ngodup gyal gyur chig - Glory to the martyr Thupten Ngodup,' the crowd cried in unison, and 'Your sacrifice shall not have been in vain.'

The eight bearers made a deep bow to the coffin on the ground. Then, wrapped in a white shroud, Thupten Ngodup's body was placed on the woodpile. More wood was added. A few juniper branches and white silk scarves were placed on top.

The watchers were very emotional. Some of them started shouting slogans once more. But most of them were crying. A few women collapsed to the ground in a faint.

Tseten Norbu approached the woodpile bearing a long flaming torch.

Those doing the policing made the crowd step back a few metres, perhaps fearing some desperate act.

For the second time flames engulfed the body — lifeless, this time — of Thupten Ngodup.

A few days after the cremation I went to meet Tseten Norbu, President of the Tibetan Youth Congress and organiser of the dramatic hunger strike at the Jantar Mantar in Delhi.

The TYC office in McLeod Ganj was on Quonium Road, about fifty metres from the bus stand. From the terrace of the office you could see the whole valley below.

Wearing a suit and tie, Tseten Norbu was a gruff-looking man with a hard-eyed gaze. It might have been the accumulated fatigue of the dramatic events of the last few days.

When I entered his room the TYC President was drinking a cup of black tea. His office was tiny. The walls were painted green. There was a colour photograph of the Dalai Lama on the wall behind him. Two large Tibetan flags were tied to ceiling-high poles.

Tseten Norbu told me, 'The hunger strike unto death organised by the Tibetan Youth Congress was simultaneously a test of our dedication to the Tibetan cause and a signal of our frustration.

'We have been here in Gandhi's country for thirty-nine years. Many countries have become independent in this period of time.

'We Tibetans are pacifists and we always put compassion first. We have used peaceful, non-violent methods in our struggle for independence. But for exactly this reason, we find ourselves very far from our objective today. And it is in this context that our hunger strike should be seen.

'With this strike we wanted to remind public opinion all over the world that for almost forty years now the Tibetans have been fighting for the freedom of their country.

'Now it is time to face the Tibetan question urgently and to concretely sustain our cause.

'When I say "concretely" I refer to the fact that, up to now, we have had strong support from groups, non-governmental organisations and the parliaments of many of the world's countries. There are mountains of declarations, resolutions, and stances in favour of the Tibetan cause. But none of this has ever been transformed into something concrete — that is to say, support of our cause by the governments of various countries.

'And the Chinese are perfectly aware of this weakness of ours.

'We wanted to send three clear messages with our hunger strike.

'First, that after almost forty years, it is imperative that leaders, politicians and governments of various countries in the world adopt a clear position in favour of Tibet.

'The second message is for the Chinese leadership. Up to now, China has interpreted the Dalai Lama's pacific and tolerant policy as a sign of weakness. If China continues to consider our struggle through peaceful means as a sign of weakness, more and more Tibetans will start trying to reach the objective of independence for Tibet through other types of struggle. We Tibetans are political refugees in India. We want to return to a free, independent Tibet. We will not have peace until we have reached this objective. The Chinese know this. With the hunger strike we wanted to tell the Chinese that Tibetans are ready to sacrifice their lives for their country, their people and their history.

'The third message is for Tibetans themselves. As I said, we have been in India for almost forty years now. But we are still very far from having achieved our objective. Today there is a mixture of complacence and resignation among Tibetans in India — complacence about the results we have obtained despite being in exile. Tibetans living in India and elsewhere in the world have a great deal more wellbeing and education today than before. Many are happy to have achieved this and are ready to renounce the fight.

'With the hunger strike, we wanted to tell these Tibetans that until we return to a free, independent Tibet, we will not have reached our objective.

'And in order to reach it, there are no shortcuts — we must be prepared for sacrifices. If we want to write a new chapter in Tibet's history, the chapter on free, independent Tibet, it can't be written without our blood and tears.'

'How do you see the sacrifice of Thupten Ngodup?' I asked.

'It's a new beginning. It's a turning point in our movement.

It is a clear message that Tibetans are ready for any sacrifice when it comes to their country, their identity and their culture. And I believe that Buddhism considers sacrificing oneself for the benefit of others, as Thupten Ngodup did, a virtue.'

I went to visit Thupten Ngodup's little house in the suburbs of McLeod Ganj together with my friend Topden.

We walked along a narrow road that ran parallel to Temple Road. There were a few stalls selling necklaces, rings, rosaries and prayer wheels. Then there was the 'Om Hotel and Restaurant', much appreciated by the young neo-hippie tourists for the scenic view from its terrace. Some ten metres on, the road was no longer tarred. It became an open latrine. Clouds of green flies rose from piles of excrement. A road made of steps began, leading steeply downwards through thick vegetation and bands of quarrelsome monkeys. Two hundred and ninety five steps later we reached the Dip Tsechokling monastery.

Thupten Ngodup's house was a tiny brick building, three and a half by two and a half metres in area. Its exterior wall adjoined one of the pavilions of the monastery. The roof was of corrugated steel. A few large rocks had been placed on the steel to stop the wind taking off the roof.

I had a rendezvous with Tenzin, one of Thupten Ngodup's friends from McLeod Ganj, in front of the house.

Tenzin was punctual. He had grey hair in a crew cut and wore a sporty blue and white striped T-shirt.

We went inside the little house.

There was a bed and a cupboard-altar in dark wood against one wall. The altar held four photographs of the Dalai Lama, pictures of other bodhisattvas, two Tibetan flags and some small brass pots for water offerings. The opposite wall had a gas stove and a shelf with pots and pans. A clothes hanger on a nail held an ironed shirt and a pair of trousers.

Tenzin was about the same age as Thupten Ngodup. When he talked about his friend his eyes occasionally filled with tears.

'We were a small group of friends,' he said. 'We were all retired soldiers. When any of us said we were too old now to do anything for the Tibetan cause, Thupten would get angry. He would say we had to fight to the very end. One day, early in March this year, Thupten invited me here to his house. He offered me some tea and told me that the next day I would have to go with him to the office of the Tibetan Youth Congress in McLeod Ganj.

'He said he wanted to take part in the "hunger strike unto death" that would begin shortly in Delhi.

'I told him it would be one of the usual demonstrations without any real results.

'He replied that this time, for once, it would be different. They had decided they were going all the way.

'The next day Thupten and I went to the office of the Tibetan Youth Congress.

'Thupten donated 500 rupees to the TYC. I was his witness. I countersigned his request to participate in the strike "unto death".

'We came back here, to the Dip Tsechokling monastery. Thupten gave me the keys to the house. He said that when I heard the news of his death I was to sell everything in here and give the money I raised to the Tibetan Youth Congress. "Every single rupee counts in carrying our struggle forward", he said.'

Thupten Ngodup was born in 1938 in Gyatso Shar in the province of Shigatse in central Tibet.

In 1959 he fled Tibet and found refuge in north-eastern India. He worked for a year on a road construction site in Bomdila. Then he moved to Bylakuppe in South India.

In April 1963 he enlisted in the Indian Army. In 1971 he took part in the military operations leading to the liberation of Bangladesh.

He retired in 1986.

In 1988 he found a job at the Dip Tsechokling monastery in McLeod Ganj, first as a herdsman and then as a cook.

In 1996 he worked for a short time as an usher in the Tibetan government in exile's Department of Security. He resigned in December the same year to take part in a peace march for the liberation of Tibet.

During the 'hunger strike unto death', while waiting for his turn, he had looked after the first six strikers.

Thupten Ngodup was a simple man. He was not especially religious. He liked drinking tea with his friends in the little 'chai-shops' in McLeod Ganj of an evening.

He was always in the front ranks of protest marches against China.

After his death he became a martyr for the Tibetans in exile - the Tibetan Jan Palach, someone said.

In the little bazaar in McLeod Ganj his photo was placed near those of the Dalai Lama and the divinities of the Buddhist pantheon. His serene face with its slightly melancholy smile appeared on postcards, posters and T-shirts.

The students of the Tibetan Children's Village of McLeod Ganj dedicated a simple remembrance to him.

They placed a large poster on the craggy mountain face that marked the boundary of their sports field. The grey silhouette of a man was drawn on it. He held his arms open and was surrounded by a large yellow flame.

The students had written on it in capital letters:

WE SALUTE OUR MARTYR THUPTEN NGODUP.

Framing the poster was a rose bush in full bloom.

Karmapa

The Tsurphu monastery was located on a hillside, like a fortified town.

The buildings to the left were painted the red of crushed grapes. On the left were the monks' small, whitewashed houses.

In the centre, topping everything else, was a pagoda-shaped gilded roof. It covered the apartments of a young monk who was only fourteen years old.

Tuesday 28th December 1999. A Mitsubishi Land cruiser had entered and left the monastery several times. Lama Tsultrim, an old lama from Tsurphu, and his assistant were to leave for the north-western part of the country to meet some of the monastery's benefactors.

The trip would be long and hard. They had loaded the vehicle with many provisions. The monastery's Chinese guards had been informed of their departure. Their travel documents were in order.

That very day, in the monastery, the fourteen-year-old lama had begun a spiritual retreat. No one was to disturb him. His spiritual master, his attendant and personal cook were the only ones to have access to his rooms.

The whole day passed in silence. Every so often there would be the ringing of prayer bells and the rhythmic beating of a drum from the young lama's room.

At seven in the evening the cook took him his dinner. It was a light meal of rice and boiled vegetables.

At 10.30 p.m. there was suddenly feverish activity in the young lama's room. The boy hurriedly changed his clothes. He had taken off his monk's clothing. He put on a pair of crumpled trousers, a heavy windcheater and a fur-lined cap with earflaps so large as to cover practically his whole face.

The youth emerged onto the terrace through a French window with his elderly attendant.

With his first jump he landed on the roof of the chapel dedicated to Mahakala.

The flame of a yak butter lamp illuminated the irate visage of the 'Great Black One,' protector of the Kagyu tradition of Tibetan Buddhism. Mahakala had a sharpened knife in his right hand and a skull cup in his left. A ring of fire surrounded his picture.

The attendant stopped for a moment to contemplate the image. 'Let's go,' the young lama said impatiently.

They climbed over one parapet, then another. Finally they found themselves hanging on to a boundary wall. They dropped to the ground.

The engine of the Mitsubishi Land Cruiser started.

Inside the car, the driver and Lama Tsultrin were seated in front. The rear seats were packed with provisions. The boot was full of cans of petrol.

The young lama and his attendant squeezed into the back among the bundles and blankets.

When the vehicle left through a side gate of the monastery the boy crouched down among the baggage.

There was no watchman. As always, at that hour the Chinese guards were all in front of the television in the refectory watching a film.

The road was in good shape. It had been tarred not long ago with donations to the monastery from followers in Taiwan. They could do the next sixty kilometres at top speed.

They came to the fork in the road leading to the Drepung monastery. Two other passengers got in — a lama, Lama Tsewang, and a second driver.

There was an important decision to be taken. Was it better

to take the northern or the southern stretch of the Friendship Highway?

The southern stretch was the busier one. Army convoys used it by day and by night. Then there were the tourist vehicles. Buses from Gonggar airport into Lhasa used the last bit of the southern stretch. A few kilometres from the airport there was a bridge over the river Yarlong Tsangpo. People's Liberation Army soldiers constantly patrolled it.

The northern stretch was better. It was longer but certainly not as constantly under surveillance.

The driver headed straight towards Yangpachen. The Chinese called it 'electricity town'. It was seventy-seven kilometres from Drepung. The six fugitives reached it at three in the morning.

At four they began climbing the Shuge La pass at an altitude of 5,350 metres. The road was good. The Mitsubishi climbed easily.

After the pass the road descended steeply to Markyang.

There was a small river — a tributary of the Yarlong Tsangpo — to be crossed.

The road started climbing again. The two drivers took turns at the wheel.

Hairpin bends. Deep ravines. The mountains were covered in snow.

Daylight was breaking by the time the Mitsubishi got to the outskirts of Detsukar. The clocks showed almost eight in the morning, Beijing time.

They crossed a bridge over the Yarlong Tsangpo. An extremely dangerous stretch of road began. It was sixty kilometres to Shigatse. The road ran parallel to the great river that took the name Brahmaputra in India. It was a good tarmac road. But it had a lot of traffic. And a lot of checkpoints.

At 9.30 a.m. they passed Nubri and its little military airport.

The young lama ducked down among the baggage in the car. But no one stopped them.

If they had been stopped, Lama Tsultirm and Lama Tsewang already had a story ready - they had 'kidnapped' the young lama.

Just before Shigaste they finally left the Friendship Highway.

They crossed the Yarlong Tsangpo once again. Now the road ran along the left bank of the river.

It was broad daylight. No one spoke inside the Mitsubishi. Everyone was thinking of Tsurphu.

In the monastery the cook had brought the young lama his breakfast. In his apartments the tutor sounded the prayer bells now and then.

Had the Chinese guards realised they had been tricked? Had they given the alarm? Maybe the omnipresent Public Security Bureau men were already hard on their heels. The driver pressed down on the accelerator as if to chase away a bad feeling.

In Shigaste they took the bypass, avoiding the city. Once again they crossed the Yarlong Tsangpo. Two young People's Liberation Army soldiers stood on the bridge. They had the red star on their fur caps and long olive-green overcoats. They were chatting. The Mitsubishi left them behind.

The scenery was magnificent. There were snow-covered mountains on the right. To the left the road skirted the river. But the six fugitives inside the Mitsubishi kept their eyes glued to the road.

They got to Lhatse at two in the afternoon.

Ten kilometres after Lhatse the road bifurcated. The driver expertly took the road to the right, without hesitating. It was the road that crossed all of western Tibet and led to the sacred Mansarovar lake.

At four in the afternoon they coasted the Ngamring Tso, a beautiful lake just outside a city of the same name.

At five they reached the small town of Sangsang. One of the drivers got down with a thermos to buy some hot tea.

Now the road ran parallel to the Raga Tsangpo river. It was tarred but full of potholes. There wasn't much traffic.

When they reached Gyerdo the first evening shadows were setting in. They were behind schedule.

They crossed Rakha. At nine p.m. it was dark as pitch. They found themselves at another fork in the road. Once again they turned right. It was a narrow, unmade road. The cold of the night stopped the dust rising. The Mitsubishi advanced slowly. It couldn't do over twenty or thirty kilometres an hour.

A little after one a.m. they reached the large town of Drongpa. They left the main road and took a small mud road. They crossed a river. The road began to climb.

At four thirty in the morning they were on the outskirts of Namashi, the last town before the frontier. The six fugitives knew there was a big military camp at Namashi.

The young lama, Lama Tsultrim and Lama Tsewang got out of the car. They carried on on foot, trying to find their way among the frozen rocks. The Mitsubishi followed at a snail's pace.

The three lamas advanced cautiously. They could not risk using an electric torch. It was several degrees below zero. Cut by the sharp stones, their hands began to bleed.

They walked for over an hour before they got back on to the dirt road. There was no trace of the Mitsubishi. Had the soldiers stopped it?

Another twenty minutes crawled by. Then they saw the Mitsubishi's low beam lights approach.

The two drivers had gone on to the border. It was unmanned.

They reversed once more. The three lamas got in quickly.

At five thirty in the morning they crossed the Kore Pass. They had entered Mustang, in Nepalese territory.

'Lha gyalo,' 'Victory to the gods,' the six fugitives said out loud. It was still pitch dark.

They waited for dawn to break near the village of Namdrol. It was a small village in the middle of a yellow scree. The road had vanished. In its place was a narrow mule track used by nomads who came to Mustang to buy sheep.

It was no longer possible to proceed with the Land Cruiser. They asked an elderly Tibetan if they could leave it parked next to the wall of his house. 'We'll come back to get it in a few days,' they said. They also asked him where they could get some horses.

It wasn't difficult to find horses in Namdrol. They hired seven horses and a guide. He asked them where they were going.

'Manang,' they replied.

They wanted to avoid the main road that led from Lo Mantang, the capital of Mustang, to Pokhara via Jomsom. It was the busiest road. There were a lot of Chinese spies among the Tibetan population of the area.

As for the Nepalese, it was better not to trust them. As a result of the accord between Nepal and the People's Republic of China, many fleeing Tibetans were handed back to the Chinese, to languish for years in the prisons of the 'Autonomous Region of Tibet'.

At this time of year the road to Manang was practically deserted. But the fugitives wanted to do it at a forced pace. They wanted to arrive in just four days.

'Impossible,' said the guide.

The fugitives got on to their horses. At two in the afternoon they reached Trenkar. They stopped outside the village to let the horses graze, and slept for four hours in the sun, wrapped in woollen blankets or curled inside sleeping bags.

When the others woke the young lama was writing something.

'I had a wonderful dream'[1], he said.

At six in the evening they were back on the move. At night the temperature dropped to well below zero. They covered the horses with blankets. At seven in the morning, starving and exhausted, they arrived at Lo Manang. They stocked up on provisions, buying bread and butter and refilling their thermoses with hot tea.

They took up their march once more.

At midday they stopped near a small river. They let the horses drink and graze and slept for a few hours.

They reached Trarang at midnight on the 31st December. The year 2000 was beginning. For the Tibetans it was just another day of the year 2126.

They walked all night, coasting the left bank of the Kali Gandaki river. The river flowed slowly between two high rocky walls.

At ten in the morning they reached Tangya and decided to rest for a few hours among the ruins of an old monastery. The hardest part of their journey awaited them. That night they would have to cross the Mustang Pass to reach Manang after another seven hours of walking.

1. The young lama later said he had dreamed of a lake lit up by the full moon. Three Brahmins dressed in white were seated on lotus flowers on the water's surface. The three priests were playing a drum, a guitar and a flute and singing a song.
When the young lama awoke he composed an aspiration for Tibet.
Like a chain of fragrant flowers
These snow-covered mountains are serene and fresh.
In a healing land,
where the white smoke of incense rises skyward,
May the precious beauty of luminous moonbeams,
light of the spiritual and temporal world,
Conquer all strife
and prevail over the darkness of its shadow side.'

They began walking once more at two in the afternoon. At midnight they started climbing Mustang Pass.

Halfway up, there was a snowstorm. They were completely blinded. The horses refused to carry on. A strong wind came down from the top of the mountain, blowing in the opposite direction to their climb. They were forced to stop and wait for the blizzard to slacken off.

At seven in the morning they crossed the pass. They were bone-weary. But they couldn't stop.

At two in the afternoon they got to Manang.

They found refuge in a tourist chalet. The young lama was feverish. His hands and feet were frost-bitten. He washed with a bucket of hot water and went to sleep.

Lama Tsewang had a 'contact' — a trustworthy friend — in Manang.

They talked for a long time on the veranda of the chalet. Then the lama drew out a bunch of banknotes from a small cloth bag inside his clothing. They were wrapped in a sheet of plastic. Dollars.

Lama Tsewang's friend left with the money. He returned in an hour. 'It's all arranged,' he said. 'Be ready at four in the afternoon.'

The helicopter arrived at four o' clock on the dot.

The six passengers got on. They had changed their clothes. But the young lama had kept his civilian clothing - a pair of trousers and a jacket. He wore a woollen cap pulled down over his eyes. A large scarf covered his mouth.

The helicopter took off. The peaks of the Annapurna range looked as if they were propping up the sky.

They landed at Nagarkot, just over an hour's drive from Kathmandu.

They hired a car to take them to Birganj on the Indian

border.

Once again they decided to travel by night. The meeting with the Nepalese driver had been fixed for midnight.

They drove fast along the Tribhuvan Highway. It went downhill all the way, and there was no traffic. At eight thirty in the morning they were at Birganj.

They took two scooter-rickshaws to cover the thirty-minute ride to the border. Lama Tsultrim and Lama Tsewang were in the second scooter with the young lama between them.

They crossed the border between Nepal and India without having to show their papers.

In another two scooters, Indian this time, they reached Raxaul Bazaar. They decided to go on to Gorakhpur in a taxi — a Maruti van. From Gorakhpur they would take a train to Delhi.

After five and a half hours on the busy Highway 28 they reached Kushinagar. Lama Tsewang murmured a prayer. The others were sleeping. Kushinagar was where the Buddha died.

At four thirty in the afternoon on the 3rd January they arrived at Gorakhpur station.

There were only a few trains going to Delhi. The seats were all booked. They decided to get on a local train. It went as far as Lucknow. It was scheduled to leave just after six in the evening. The train arrived very late and was incredibly crowded. They pushed their way into a second class carriage. It was a long, tiring trip. The train stopped at every station. They reached Lucknow after midnight.

It was impossible to carry on travelling in such conditions. They decided they would go to Delhi by car, and hired another Maruti van.

Although it was the dead of night there were a lot of trucks at full speed on Highway 24. They were coming from the opposite direction, and avoided the Maruti van at the last minute. The Tibetan sitting next to the driver began reciting the mantra 'Om mani padme hum,' until he fell asleep.

Sitapur. Shahjanpur. Bareilly. Rampur. Moradabad. Hapur. Ghaziabad. And then the squalid outskirts of the Indian capital.

At two in the afternoon on the 4th January they were in Delhi.

The young lama was impatient. He was in a hurry to reach McLeod Ganj.

They hired two white Ambassadors.

At four in the afternoon, before they left, the young lama dialled a number on his mobile phone. It was seven in the evening in Tsurphu. Dinner time. 'Hello. We've reached Delhi,' the young lama said, and disconnected.

In the room on the top floor of the Tsurphu monastery, the tutor and the cook had eight hours in which to disappear without trace.

At five in the evening the two white Ambassadors left for Ambala. Despite the intense traffic it was possible to travel quite fast on National Highway 1. They went from Ambala to Ludhiana without stopping.

At Jalandhar they left Highway 1 and took Highway 1A in the direction of Pathankot. And then up to Dharamsala and McLeod Ganj.

At ten thirty on the morning of the 5th January they walked up the small path leading to the entrance of the Hotel Bhagsu. Although it was winter, the roses were in bloom.

They asked for three rooms. They signed in as 'Lama Tsultrim and Party' on the hotel register. They were extremely tired and would show their papers later.

Lama Tsewang telephoned a friend who lived in McLeod Ganj. He asked for Tashi Wangdi's telephone number.

Tashi Wangdi was a 'kalon', a minister of the Tibetan government in exile. He was minister for religious and cultural affairs.

'I'll send my secretary across right now,' Tashi Wangdi said, and put the 'phone down.

When he reached the Hotel Bhagsu the minister's secretary asked to see the young lama. When he saw him he couldn't hide his amazement. He rang Tashi Wangdi immediately. The minister in his turn rang the Dalai Lama's personal secretary.

'An important reincarnated lama has arrived,' he announced. 'I must speak to His Holiness urgently.'

'He is on a retreat. His Holiness cannot speak to anyone,' was the reply.

The minister didn't give up. He told the secretary the name of the young lama who had just arrived.

There was a moment of silence.

The secretary came back on the line.

'His Holiness asks that he be brought here immediately.'

In McLeod Ganj, the road leading to the Main Temple was blocked by snow. The little group had to walk the distance of one kilometre from the Hotel Bhagsu to the Dalai Lama's residence. Tashi Wangdi was at the gate of the residence to meet them.

They were searched. The young lama was now wearing his monk's clothing.

They walked up another small stretch. Then the young lama saw the Dalai Lama for the first time in his life, waiting on the veranda of his modest house. He had a long white silk scarf in his hands.

'You must be very tired,' the Dalai Lama said to the boy.

'Yes,' he replied, smiling.

Tenzin Gyatso, the fourteenth Dalai Lama of Tibet, and Ogyen Trinley Dorje, the seventeenth Karmapa, were now facing each other. It was a meeting destined to enter the pages of the history of modern Tibet.

***

The 'Gyalwa Karmapa' is the spiritual head of the Kagyu tradition, one of the four big schools of Tibetan Buddhism.

The Kagyu tradition traces its origins to the Buddha Shakyamuni. Marpa, the 'Great Translator,' is the central figure of the Kagyu. Marpa went to India thrice to bring the original teachings of the Buddha back to Tibet. Naropa was Marpa's teacher. Tilopa was Naropa's teacher. And so on, back to the historic Buddha.

Marpa's most famous disciple was Milarepa, an ascetic, yogi and saint. Milarepa passed the teachings to Gampopa who, in his turn, transferred them to Dusum Khyenpa (1110-1193), the first Karmapa.

Since then the Kagyu lineage has come down to our days without interruption.

This particular lineage is called 'self-announced' because each Karmapa leaves a letter in which he foresees his own reincarnation.

The Gyalwa Karmapas were proof of one of the Buddha Shakyamuni's prophecies. During his earthly existence, in fact, the Buddha said that a 'fully developed teacher' would reappear in the form of Karmapa.

The Gyalwa Karmapa, 'teacher of karma,' 'he who carries out the activity of a Buddha,' is also viewed as an emanation of Avalokiteswara, the Bodhisattva of Compassion. The Karmapa manifests himself in this world to alleviate human suffering. He distributes alms, heals the sick, preaches and builds monasteries.

After the Dalai Lama and the Panchen Lama, the Gyalwa Karmpa is Tibet's third spiritual head.

Rangjung Rigpe Dorje was the sixteenth Karmapa. He too lived in the Tsurphu monastery 70 kilometres to the northwest of Lhasa.

The first Karmapa, Dusum Khyenpa, founded the monastery in 1189. Since then the monastery has been the seat of all the successive Karmapas.

After the Chinese occupation of Tibet in 1959 the sixteenth Karmapa went into exile in Rumtek, a small town 24 kilometres from Gangtok, the capital of Sikkim. Sikkim was then a small independent Himalayan state.

The sixteenth Karmapa carried the famous 'Vajra Mukut' or 'black cap' with him to Rumtek. Tai Ming Yunglo, the second emperor of the Ming dynasty, had given the cap to the fifth Karmapa, Debzhing Sherpa. It is said that this cap was made from strands of the hair of the Dakinis or celestial messengers. The Vajra Mukut was also called 'flying cap'. When the Karmapa placed it on his head, he kept it in place with his right hand.

In exile, the sixteenth Karmapa gave the Kagyu tradition new impetus. In 1966 he finished building the Rumtek monastery. He also founded over 430 centres of Tibetan Buddhism all over the world.

When the Karmapa died of cancer in Zion, Illinois on the 5th November 1981, he left property worth one billion two hundred million dollars.

The seventeenth Karmapa would be his sole heir.

When an important 'tulku' or reincarnated lama died, strong religious, political and economic interests came into play. The identification of the new reincarnation often led to heated arguments.

When the sixteenth Karmapa died, his four 'sons of the heart' - his four major disciples - placed themselves at the head of the Kagyu order while waiting to identify the new reincarnation of their spiritual leader.

The four regents were Kunzing Shamar, Tai Situ, Jamgon

Kongtrul and Goshir Gyaltsab. All four were reincarnated lamas. They were better known as Shamar Rinpoche (or Shamarpa), Tai Situ Rinpoche, Jamgon Kongtrul Rinpoche and Gyaltsab Rinpoche. This was also their hierarchical order within the Kagyu order.

Almost immediately, there was a split between Shamar Rinpoche on the one hand and Tai Situ and Gyaltsab Rinpoche on the other.

Besides being the first in the Kagyu hierarchy after the Karmapa, Shamar Rinpoche was also the nephew of the sixteenth Karmapa. Hence he wished to personally identify the child in whom the deceased Karmapa would be reincarnated.

But the figure of the Shamar Rinpoche had been very controversial in Tibet over the past centuries.

Towards the middle of the 1600s, the Kagyu order had gone through a strong revival in the Kham province of eastern Tibet as a result of the untiring work of the eighth Tai Situ.

A century later, the Shamar Rinpoche tried to do likewise in central Tibet. In order to reach his objective he allied himself with his brother, the Panchen Lama, who belonged to the Gelug tradition. The Panchen Lama of the time had disagreed strongly with the Dalai Lama and the rest of the yellow-cap hierarchy.

The new alliance between the Shamar Rinpoche and the Panchen Lama preoccupied the Gelug establishment. The Panchen Lama was sent to Beijing, where he died in mysterious circumstances.

Having lost the protection of his powerful brother, the Shamar Rinpoche fled to Nepal. He was accused of plotting against Tibet. When war broke out immediately after between the two Himalayan countries, the Shamar Rinpoche was declared a traitor.

He was officially forbidden to reincarnate himself. All his possessions were confiscated. His closest collaborators were put in prison.

But for over two hundred years, despite the mantras recited against him, the Shamar Rinpoche continued to secretly reincarnate himself.

It was only at the beginning of the twentieth century that the figure of the Shamar Rinpoche was reinstated when, in order to strengthen Tibetan national unity, the thirteenth Dalai Lama abolished many of the laws that punished the rival Kagyu order.

The current — fourteenth — Dalai Lama, who was friends with the sixteenth Karmapa, abolished the ban on the reincarnation of the Shamar Rinpoche that had lasted for over two centuries.

This reinstatement had strong repercussions within the Kagyu order.

When the sixteenth Karmapa died, Shamar on the one hand, and Situ and Gyaltsab on the other, began their covert struggle for control of his reincarnation.

The fourth regent, Jamgon Kongtrul Rinpoche, avoided assuming a clear position, keeping himself relatively neutral in regard to the two warring factions. Later, when the struggle began to include low blows, Jamgon Kongtrul Rinpoche died in a road accident. His powerful BMW 525 crashed into a tree near Siliguri, a small town in West Bengal, India.

The Kagyu tradition introduced the 'tulku' system in Tibet. When a Karmapa was still alive he would write a letter in which he would set out precise indications on finding the child in whom he would be reincarnated. So where was the sixteenth Karmapa's letter?

On the morning of the 19th March 1992 the four regents met in the Rumtek monastery in Sikkim. Tai Situ Rinpoche told the other three that he had news that was 'as joyful as the peacock's cry.' He had found the letter containing the sixteenth Karmapa's prediction.

He told this story: 'In Calcutta, a few months before he died, His Holiness the sixteenth Karmapa gave me a protective amulet. "This will be very useful to you in the future," he told me. The amulet was in some brocade wrapping. I always had it around my neck on a cord. One day in the summer of 1989 I decided to replace the cord, which was fraying. As I was doing so the amulet opened. There was a small envelope folded inside it. On the envelope was written: "To be opened in the Year of the Iron Horse"[2].

'I opened the envelope at the indicated time. There was a letter of prediction inside.'

Tai Situ Rinpoche distributed copies of the letter to the three other regents assembled at Rumtek that morning. The letter read:

> 'Self-awareness is always bliss.
> Emptiness has neither centre nor edge.
> From here to the north, then the east of the Land of Snows,
> Is a country where divine thunder spontaneously blazes[3]
> In a beautiful nomad's place with the sign of the cow[4],
> The labour is Dondrub and the wisdom is Lolaga[5].
> Born in the year of the one who works the earth[6]

2. The year 1990.
3. The region in which the seventeenth Karmapa was born is called Lhathok. 'Lha' means 'divinity', 'divine'. 'Thok' means thunder.
4. The name of the place in which the Karmapa was born is Baor. 'Ba' means cow.
5. 'Labour' refers to the father, 'wisdom' to the mother.
6. 'The one who works the earth' is the ox. The Karmapa was born in 1985, year of the wooden ox for the Tibetans.

Announced by the miraculous sound of the white
conch shell[7],
This is the one known as Karmapa.'

Gyaltsab Rinpoche and Jagmon Kongtrul Rinpoche immediately gave their approval. At the sight of the precious letter Gyaltsab prostrated himself before it with tears in his eyes.

Shamar Rinpoche merely said, 'I think it's a fake.'

He asked for a handwriting analysis. Tai Situ Rinpoche refused.

On the 17th May 1992, Tai Situ Rinpoche and Gyaltsab Rinpoche announced in Rumtek that their two representatives Akong Tulku and Sherab Tharchin had left for Tibet. They were to find the new reincarnation of the Kagyu tradition's spiritual leader in accordance with the instructions in the sixteenth Karmapa's letter of prediction.

It was not a difficult task. They found the child. He had been born into a family of nomads in the Tibetan region of Lhathok in 1985.

When the news reached him Tai Situ communicated it to the Dalai Lama who was on a visit to Brazil.

The Dalai Lama confirmed the identification.

On the 27th June 1992 the Chinese government too officially recognised the new Karmapa. They gave him the title 'Living Buddha'.

When the Dalai Lama returned from Brazil he gave Tai Situ Rinpoche an official letter confirming the new reincarnation[8].

---

7. This refers to the sound of the conch that was mysteriously heard for about an hour immediately after the Karmapa was born.
8. The 'Buktham Rinpoche,' the 'Precious Letter', reads:
'The boy born to Karma Dondrub and Lolaga in the Wood Ox year, identified by

With this letter in hand Tai Situ Rinpoche returned to the Rumtek monastery in Sikkim.

At the monastery there was a lot of tension. The monks were divided into two factions, one in favour of Tai Situ Rinpoche and the other for Shamar Rinpoche.

Acts of vandalism had already taken place. Physical violence now followed. More than once, Indian policemen and soldiers had to intervene.

The situation was getting out of hand as far as Shamar Rinpoche was concerned. He had to identify an alternative Karmapa. He found him in Lhasa, the capital of Tibet.

The child lived in the Barkor. He was the son of Mipham Rinpoche, a lama of the Nyingma tradition.

Shamar Rinpoche hastened to organise the child's departure from Tibet.

In 1994 his parents requested a tourist visa for Kathmandu. The Chinese authorities gave it to them. Once they were in Nepal, it was not difficult for Mipham Rinpoche's family to carry on to Delhi.

On the 27th January 1994, Shamar Rinpoche officially announced in New Delhi that the new reincarnation of the Karmapa had been found.

The release read, 'I, Shamar Rinpoche, announce that the authentic reincarnation of the sixteenth Karmapa, Ranjung Rigpe Dorje, has been identified. The seventeenth Karmapa is currently in India. More details on the traditional enthronement ceremony will follow.'

The child was given the name Trinley Thaye Dorje.

The enthronement ceremony was fixed for the 17th March 1994 at the Karmapa Buddhist Institute in New Delhi.

the prediction letter, is hereby recognised as the reincarnation of the sixteenth Karmapa. With prayers for his well-being and the success of his activities. The Dalai Lama. The third day of the fourth Tibetan month in the Water Monkey Year, June 3rd 1992.'

Fearing trouble, Shamar Rinpoche had 'his' Karmapa arrive the evening before the ceremony. The official guests arrived on the morning of the 17th March.

Tai Situ Rinpoche's men were at the Institute from the early hours of the day. Several monks in front of the gate were chanting slogans against Shamar Rinpoche and his 'Puppet Karmapa.'

As the demonstrators shouted slogans, a black Mercedes emerged from the main gate of the Institute. It was Shamar Rinpoche's idea. To distract the attention of the demonstrators, he made it appear that the Mercedes was going to pick up the child and bring him to the Institute.

Meanwhile, inside the Karmapa Buddhist Institute, the ceremony was in full swing. When the demonstrators realised they had been tricked they tried to break down the door.

Twenty monks stormed the Institute. Others pelted stones at them to drive them back.

The two sides began an intense stone-throwing session. The windows of the Institute were shattered. The battle went on for about half an hour. Nine people were arrested. Several were wounded. One of them ended up in hospital with a smashed skull.

Shamar Rinpoche said he had proof that since 1991 Tai Situ Rinpoche had known the child he later indicated as being the new Karmapa. In fact, that year he had visited the Kalek monastery where the young 'Apo Gaga' was a novice.

Shamar Rinpoche said that once he had chosen the child, Tai Situ had written the false letter of prediction indicating the birthplace of the new Karmapa and the names of his parents.

Shamar Rinpoche also said that the 'Chinese Karmapa' was a 'threat to the safety of India.' The 'Shamarpa' recalled that China has never accepted India's annexation of Sikkim in 1975. A Karmapa loyal to the Chinese in Rumtek could be a serious risk to Indian sovereignty in the sensitive border zone.

Shamar Rinpoche's war continued on the Internet — it was www.karmapa.org (Trinley Thaye Dorje) versus www.kagyu.org (Ogyen Trinley Dorje).

But Shamar Rinpoche's weapons had been blunted. By now, as a result of the Dalai Lama's 'Precious Letter', Ogyen Trinley Dorje was the real Karmapa.

The Chinese government recognised Ogyen Trinley Dorje as the seventeenth Karmapa 24 days after the date on the Dalai Lama's 'Precious Letter'. It was the first time the Chinese Communist Party had 'approved' the identification of an incarnate lama.

At dawn on the 2nd August 1992, a solemn ceremony was held in the Jokhang in Lhasa. The fringe of the child identified as the new Karmapa was cut off in front of the statue of Jowo Shakyamuni. He was given the name Pal Kyabdak Ogyen Gyalway Nguyu Drodul Trinely Dorje Tsal Chokle Nampar Gyalway De.

Many Communist Party officials of the Autonomous Region of Tibet were present at the Johkang.

On the 27th September 1992, the investiture ceremony was held in the Tsurphu monastery. Some 20,000 followers from all over the world had rushed to be there. The Chinese deputy minister for religious affairs had arrived from Beijing.

The *People's Daily* of the 22nd June 1993 published an in-depth article on the young Karmapa. It said, 'The young Buddha is very serious in the presence of the teacher. When the teacher leaves he becomes a normal child once again, playing with his toys. All his followers hope he will become a patriotic "Living Buddha".'

The same month, the Chinese delegate at the Conference on Human Rights being held in Vienna said, 'The young

Karmapa, *the future successor of the Dalai Lama* (Author's italics), is preparing to be able to take on all his responsibilities in Tibet one day.'

It appeared, therefore, that the Chinese government was focusing on the young Karmapa.

In September 1994 Ogyen Trinley Dorje was officially invited to Beijing.

On the 1st October he took part in the forty-fifth anniversary celebrations of the proclamation of the People's Republic of China. On this occasion the Karmapa, a nine-year-old child, met the president Jiang Zemin and the president of the National Assembly Li Peng.

The *People's Daily* reported the news of the meetings, writing, 'The "Living Buddha" Karmapa said that he will study hard and always follow the directives of the Chinese Communist Party.' The 'paper also said the little Karmapa had shouted 'Long live the People's Republic of China' at the end of each meeting.

Early in December 1995, the Karmapa was taken to the Tashilhunpo monastery in Shigatse. He was made to take part in the ceremony to enthrone Gyaltsen Norbu, the Panchen Lama the Chinese had chosen.

In January 1999, Ogyen Trinley Dorje went to Beijing for the second time.

Once again the 'patriotic Karmapa' met the leaders of the People's Republic of China. They pressurised him to publicly denounce the Dalai Lama. He refused to do so. 'How can I denounce him when I don't even know him?' he said.

At the end of his visit *China's Tibet* magazine published an article in which it stated that the 'Living Buddha' had 'prayed for the spirit of Mao Zedong' and quoted him as saying he wanted to 'follow the teachings of President Jiang Zemin.' Once he returned to Tsurphu, he would 'undertake to build a prosperous and united Tibet' and 'always love China.'

But something had happened a few months earlier. Two Chinese men had tried to assassinate the young Karmapa at Tsurphu. They had been caught hiding under blankets in the library of the monastery. They were armed with knives and a rudimentary hand grenade.

The library of the monastery led to the Karmapa's rooms on the third floor of the building.

The Karmapa had been absent from his rooms at the time. He was on a picnic with other monks two kilometres from Tsurphu. Although it had begun to rain, the Karmapa had said he didn't want to return to the monastery because he had a 'bad feeling.'

The two Chinese confessed to having been paid by someone in Lhasa to murder the Karmapa. The monks handed them over to the Chinese authorities. But the two were released after a few days.

It was then that Ogyen Trinley Dorje began to think about escaping.

In McLeod Ganj, the young Karmapa moved from the Hotel Bhagsu to the Chonor Guest House.

A few days later he went to live in the Gyuto Ramoche monastery in Sidhbari about twenty kilometres from McLeod Ganj, where armed policemen guarded him day and night.

Meanwhile, in the Tsurphu monastery the flight had been discovered and the Chinese repression had begun. The monastery was closed to the public. There were searches, interrogations and arrests. Ogyen Trinley Dorje's own parents were moved from Lhasa to Chamdo in eastern Tibet and placed under house arrest there.

The Karmapa's escape strained diplomatic relations between China and India.

Zho Bangzao, the spokesman for the Chinese Ministry of

External Affairs, said that if India granted the Karmapa political asylum it would be violating the 'Panchsheel' or 'Five Principles', the basis of peaceful coexistence between the two countries.

A few days later, Zhou Gang, the Chinese ambassador in New Delhi, asked the Indian government 'not to use the presence of the seventeenth Karmapa to endorse anti-Chinese activities in India.'

It didn't take the young Karmapa long to voice his own ideas.

On the 4th February 2000, exactly one month after his arrival in India, he said at the Gyuto monastery: 'Freedom is necessary in order to practise Buddhism's fundamental teaching, compassion.'

On the 19th February 2000, the sixtieth anniversary of the investiture of the fourteenth Dalai Lama was celebrated at the 'Tipa' (Tibetan Institute of Performing Arts) in McLeod Ganj.

The young Karmapa made his first public speech in India.

He said, 'There are conflicts due to lack of freedom and the violation of human rights in many countries in the world. Let's take the case of our country. Tibet used to be the country in which the Buddhist faith flowered in every field, both spiritual and intellectual. Tibet has suffered a great deal in the last forty years. Today, Tibetan religion, culture and traditions risk being wiped out forever.'

In the beginning the Chinese wire service Xinhua had reported that the Karmapa had gone to India to carry the 'black cap' and some musical instruments from the Rumtek monastery in Sikkim back to Tsurphu.

The truth was that the Karmapa had run away.

Ogyen Trinley Dorje was destined to assume a role of major importance within the Tibetan community in exile after the death of the present Dalai Lama and in the interim before his successor would become an adult.

***

I visited the Tantric monastery of Gyuto one Sunday morning. Winter was almost over and the sun was shining in McLeod Ganj.

In the bazaar's two parallel lanes, roadside stalls had occupied the space in front of the shops, which were closed for the holiday. The stalls were selling many of colourful goods — clothes, woollen pullovers, handicrafts and religious pictures.

There was a small photographer's shop, 'Choice Studio', on Temple Road. The owner had placed a little wooden table with colour photos of the Karmapa on it out on the road. There was one of the Dalai Lama and the Karmapa shaking hands in front of a picture of Avalokiteshwara. The photo had been taken in the Dalai Lama's residence the day the young lama arrived in McLeod Ganj. There was another photo of the Karmapa in sunglasses at the Tibetan Institute of Performing Arts during the sixtieth anniversary celebrations of the Dalai Lama's investiture. There were close-up shots of the fourteen-year-old lama's serious face.

The taxi stand was at the end of Temple Road. I negotiated a price to Sidhbari.

'Come here after?' the taxi driver asked me in halting English.

'Yes,' I replied. We agreed on a price and he started his car.

Then he threw it at breakneck speed onto the road that went down to Dharamsala. The road was full of potholes and the Maruti van left a thick cloud of yellowish dust behind it.

In Kotwali Bazaar the traffic was at a standstill. There was a frenzy of horn blowing. A long line of jeeps and military trucks stood waiting.

Once out of Dharamsala the Maruti took up its race once

more. The suburbs of the town looked like one big garbage dump. We crossed a small cement bridge. The river flowed sinuously through a green valley.

A few kilometres on, buildings began to reappear by the roadside — a 'chai shop', a sweetshop, a chemist's with a colourful signboard, a tailor's, a greengrocer's.

A cobbler sat in the shade of a large banyan tree.

I spotted a yellow sign on the side of the road with 'GYUTO TANTRIC MONASTERY. SIDHBARI' written on it in red in Tibetan and English.

I went up a small gravel road and found myself in front of a large flight of stairs leading into the monastery.

Halfway up the stairs was a stone slab with a plaque: 'Inaugurated by the Dalai Lama on the third day of the tenth month of 2123, Year of the Fire Rat.'

A Tibetan flag flew from the roof of the building.

There were armed policemen on guard.

There was an audience scheduled at two in the afternoon.

Several Tibetans were already there waiting, telling their beads and reciting mantras. Their muttering was drowned by the sound of crows cawing.

At a quarter to two the foreign visitors were asked to assemble under a neem tree. A guard wrote our names in a register and checked our passports. There were ten of us — an Irish couple, a Frenchwoman, an Austrian man, two Americans, an Israeli woman, a South Korean woman and a Taiwanese man.

We entered the large hall of the monastery. It was cold. We sat cross-legged on sea green mats.

There was a big gold-plated statue of the Buddha Shakyamuni before us. The Buddha too was sitting cross-legged. His right hand touched the ground and he was scowling.

In front of the statue was an altar. There was a colour

photograph of the Dalai Lama on it. There was a redwood throne in front of the altar.

The stairs leading to the throne had a bas-relief of the two 'golden fish' with the wheel of Dharma in the centre. The fish represented the liberation of the mind from the ocean of samsara.

The Karmapa arrived at twenty to three. Three monks accompanied him.

His plainclothes Indian guards lined up behind him, grim-faced. They stood with legs apart, their hands behind their backs.

The Karmapa smiled. He was very tall. He looked older than fourteen. His face was round, like the full moon. He had slanting eyes and thick lips. Ogyen Trinley Dorje started his teaching.

His voice was that of a boy. In the beginning, he groped for words. A monk translated his Tibetan.

The seventeenth Karmapa said: 'Thank you all for having come here. My special thanks to those who have come from far away.

'We find the teachings of the Buddha in the Sutras and the Tantras.

'Compassion, a good heart, kindness and a bodhicitta or truly altruistic aptitude are the fundamental teachings of Buddhism.

'Being Buddhist means taking refuge in the "Three Jewels" — the Buddha, the Dharma and the Sangha.

'Once we have taken refuge in the Buddha, we should no longer seek refuge in worldly gods.

'Once we have taken refuge in Dharma, we must no longer hurt living beings.

'Taking refuge in the Sangha is like making a good friend who will show us the right way and stop us doing negative things.

'Dedicating our lives to the Three Jewels is like crossing a river. The Buddha is the other side, the place we want to reach. Dharma is our boat. The Sangha is our boatman.

'Through the Three Jewels we can reach complete enlightenment.

'But once we have understood the importance of the Three Jewels and a bodhicitta aptitude, we must behave accordingly.'

The fourteen-year-old lama tried to be more convincing on this last point. He concluded with a comparison. 'Otherwise,' he said, 'it would be like having a powerful car and always keeping it locked up in the garage.'

We all lined up to offer 'His Holiness' a khata, the white silk scarf.

In exchange we would receive a ribbon of red satin tied with a knot. It was the blessing of the Karmapa.

The devout who preceded me made many prostrations and bows. When it was my turn, I greeted Ogyen Trinley Dorje with a simple handshake.

'Congratulations,' I told him.

The seventeenth Karmapa shook my hand with equal vigour. His slanting eyes were full of laughter.

Lingkor

The seat number on my boarding card for flight SZ 408 was 18A.

The faces of the China Southwest Airlines stewardesses looked as if they were made of porcelain. Their eyebrows had been drawn on with a thin pencil. Their mouths were small and heavily lipsticked. They wore their hair tied back in black velvet hairnets. They said 'Good morning' without the shadow of a smile.

At ten past ten the Boeing 757 began taxiing along the runway at Kathmandu's Tribhuvan airport.

As soon as we had taken off the captain informed us that Lhasa was six hundred kilometres from Kathmandu. It would be a fifty-minute flight.

We flew over a sandy plateau with no signs of life.

The clouds looked like cotton balls floating in mid air. They cast round shadows, the colour of charcoal, on the ground.

The captain announced that we were nearing Mount Everest. All the passengers moved to the left of the plane.

The hostesses served a snack — a cold mini-pizza and a glass of tepid Sprite.

An emerald green lake, set into the mountainside like a precious stone, disappeared beneath us.

We flew over a range of pointed black mountain peaks. They looked like the waves of some raging sea.

The plane began its descent. Underneath us the riverbed of the Yarlong Tsangpo could be seen.

The landing was abrupt. 'We have arrived at Gongkar airport in Lhasa,' a female voice announced over the PA system.

In just a few minutes, I would be on the sacred soil of Tibet.

I had decided to come to Lhasa because I wanted to walk the Lingkor, the 'sacred way' that circles the city.

I mentioned it to the unavoidable tourist guide I had been assigned.

'Impossible,' was the immediate response from Sonam, a short Tibetan with a crew cut and a permanent smile on his lips.

I telephoned Mrs. Shao, the Chinese lady who ran the travel agency.

'Foreigners are not allowed access to the eastern part of the city,' Mrs. Shao explained.

I replied that I had only come to Lhasa to do the circuit of the Lingkor. I said I would do it anyway, even without permission. 'No one can keep me prisoner in my hotel,' I announced in an intentionally theatrical tone of voce.

Mrs. Shao asked me to let her speak to the tourist guide.

They had a long conversation in Chinese. Then the man hung up.

'Tomorrow we walk all around the Linkgor,' Sonam said, without his usual smile. 'But no cameras,' he added.

The idea of going to Lhasa to walk around the Lingkor had come to me while reading F. Spencer Chapman's book, *Lhasa the Holy City*. The book had been published in London in 1938.

Spencer Chapman went to Lhasa in July 1936. He was part of the British government mission in Lhasa headed by B.J. Gould. He returned to Calcutta in February 1937.
On the 6th July 2003, the Dalai Lama's sixty-eighth birthday, I walked the entire length of Lhasa's Lingkor.

I had a photocopy of the pages from Spencer Chapman's book about the 'sacred way' in my pocket.

I

Yesterday.

F. Spencer Chapman writes: 'In part of the Cathedral buildings there is a religious cloister, the circuit of which must be made at frequent intervals by the devout. In the course of this perambulation several hundred prayer wheels, set in racks almost touching each other, must be turned. There is also an intermediate circle around the block of buildings of which the Cathedral forms the centre. Enormous prayer-poles surmounted by yaks' tails and chortens mark the course of this circuit. The third and outer circle runs right round the entire city and Potala. It is called the Lingkor or "park circle". All Buddhists are supposed to go round this each day, especially on holy days, the fifteenth and last of each month. And as to walk round it gives one a glimpse of many sides of Lhasa life, I will describe the circuit in some detail.

'The Sacred Way runs past the square mud-brick archway leading out of the Deyki Lingka. We have to turn left because the circuit must be made in a clockwise direction; prayer wheels are also turned in this way, and when chortens are encountered they must be passed on the right hand side. To do these things in the reverse direction would stamp one as an adherent of the Bon religion, and would nullify the good work of others.

'As we meet the Lhasa-Norbhu Lingka road at right angles there is a pile of stones marking the spot from which the Potala again becomes visible. On the other side of the road are sitting two or three beggars, clad in patchwork garments of filthy rags and wearing necklaces composed of fragments of conch-shell bracelets. Along the main road comes a gang of coolie women carrying along block of granite to be used in the building of some nobleman's house. As they walk they chant a peculiar and monotonous dirge to keep in step. Sometimes these stones are carried on a wooden two-wheeled cart — the only wheeled vehicle used in Lhasa.'

Spencer Chapman writes that the Lingkor is only three metres wide here. It runs between walls of sun-dried brick. Beyond the walls are groves of white poplar and willow.

Spencer Chapman comes across a pilgrim prostrating himself. 'We overtake a man who is measuring his length round the Sacred Way. As the total distance is between eight and nine kilometres he must make nearly 3,000 obeisances per circuit. This man has short hair but does not wear monk's dress. He has a long leather apron strapped over his front and wears on his feet wooden clogs protected with heavy iron nails. He stands with his feet together muttering prayers, brings his hands together in front of him, then lies flat on his face with his arms stretched out beyond his head. He stands up, brings his hands together again, and then walks forward to the point reached by his hands. Sometimes he stops to rest by the road, marking his progress with a small stone. Unless he is a very notable sinner, I don't think he is doing this on his own account, as I see him at work almost every day. Probably he is wiping out the transgressions of some high official — for a consideration. These exalted people excuse themselves from this form of devotion on the grounds that their presence would distract the other worshippers.'

The sacred road coasts the sandy bank of the aqueduct of Lhasa and the road to India. 'The Lingkor, here little more than a couple of metres wide, is constructed by an outcrop of rock. This is being gradually scraped away as it is a remedy for rheumatism if taken internally. It is very sandy here, and fifty or sixty bright-plumaged sacred cocks attached to the Chinese temple strut about in the road.'

Chapman is not alone on the Lingkor. 'Looking back, I can see as many as fifty people following; practically all are turning prayer wheels or telling their beads. There are very few young people and few men. Old women predominate. It is only when their time in this life becomes short that they seriously start to prepare themselves for the next. Some of these women lead small dogs which look like crosses between Lhasa terriers and Chinese spaniels.'

The Lingkor crosses marshy terrain and forests of weeping willow to arrive at the famous Snake Temple.

'The temple was considered by the Chinese to be one of the five beauties of Lhasa. We visited it soon after we arrived.

'There is a causeway of ancient poplar logs, but in September it was submerged and a ragged boatman was there to ferry us across to some stone steps that come down to the water's edge. Watching the many-hued dragonflies and looking across the untroubled surface of the lake to where the iridescent heads of the mallard drakes scintillate among the bowing rushes, and behind them to the luxuriant willows, it is difficult to believe we are nearly 3,700 metres above sea level.

'In the shade of an enormous poplar is the temple, small and square-roofed, with a curious hexagonal tiled dome and a conventional conical ornament on the summit. Hanging from the six corners of the roof are gilt dragons with raised elephantine trunks; from each a golden bell is suspended with a piece of flat metal attached to the clapper so that they tinkle in the wind. Behind the temple lies the northern escarpment of the Potala, somewhat foreshortened from here but as impressive as ever.

'The temple, like so many Tibetan shrines, is disappointing inside, nor are there any snakes - at any rate not live ones, though some of the idols have diadems or necklaces of writhing serpents. There is, however, a small chamber with a divan where the Dalai Lama used to come and meditate for hours together.

'This temple is the abode of a most powerful demon who is the spirit of the lake on which the city of Lhasa is built. On a certain day of each year all the officials and people of Lhasa must visit the temple in order to propitiate him. Having walked in procession around the city the Prime Minister and the Shappes, dressed in their yellow silk robes, and other officials in all their finery, must present scarves to the water-spirit.'

Today.

I began my walk along the sacred way at the point at which the Lingkor met the Norbulingka Lu. At the end of this road the Potala's western flank appeared on the right. Its walls were garnet red, its roofs golden. The encircling rampart, tapered at the top, was painted white. The boundary walls of the imposing building climbed the slopes of the Marpo Ri.

The Dalai Lama's residence looked like a big boat that had run aground on the rocks after a shipwreck.

Perspiring Tibetan workers wearing straw hats were tarring the Norbulingka Lu. Chinese foremen were supervising the work. A large yellow cement mixer blocked the road.

There was a five storey building in a hybrid Chinese style across the road. It had blue-tinted glass doors and a high, asymmetrical tower on the right, its roof and pagoda covered in red brick. The building was the Traffic Department Office.

I crossed the Norbulingka Lu, keeping an eye on the freshly laid tar.

Along this stretch the Lingkor was a small, unmade road, squeezed between two whitewashed walls. To the left was a grove of poplar and weeping willow. To the right were the single-family villas of high ranking officials of the Autonomous Region of Tibet and the Chinese Communist Party.

A few metres on I went past the road leading to the Kunde Ling monastery.

It was one of Lhasa's four 'royal' monasteries. During the Cultural Revolution the Red Guards had razed it to the ground.

Now the Lingkor ran along the base of the Bompo Ri. There was a temple to Gesar, the legendary hero from eastern Tibet, on top of the hill.

The beeping of car horns and the roar of traffic called my attention to the Beijing Zhonglu, Central Beijing Road.

Before crossing the big tree-lined avenue, I saw a few

pilgrims on their knees at the base of the Bompo Ri.

I went closer. The prie-dieu, worn to a shine from use, was a hollow in a slab of black flint stuck between the blocks of granite at the foot of the hill. The devout had heaped round white stones near the prie-dieu.

A few feet away the Lhasa municipality had constructed a cube-shaped edifice covered with shiny white tiles. It housed the public toilets of the Beijing Zhonglu. The attendant, a middle-aged Chinese woman, was sitting on a metal folding stool, knitting.

At ten-thirty in the morning there was intense traffic on the Beijing Zhonglu. There were big Volkswagen 'Santana' taxis, manufactured in China. Toyota jeeps. Dong Feng military trucks. Motorcycles. Bicycles. In 1959 Lhasa's area was less than three square kilometres. Forty years later the Tibetan capital spread over 25 square kilometres.

The population had gone from 30,000 to 200,000. Seventy per cent of the people were Han Chinese-soldiers, policemen, Communist Party members, white-collar workers, technicians and construction workers. Above all, there was a growing number of shopkeepers.

When I visited Lhasa it had 13,000 businesses. Only three hundred of them were managed by Tibetans.

I crossed the Beijing Zhonglu near the Hotel Shne Diya.

It was an imposing building with a moss green glass façade and a black marble staircase leading to the entry. The name of the hotel was written in Chinese characters in bronze, fixed onto the large glass windows. The rest of the structure was made of red brick. The window and doorframes had been painted white.

I continued my walk along the tree-lined avenue. There was no trace of the old Lingkor.

There were low two-storeyed buildings along the pavement - shops, their names written on big red signboards in Chinese characters. There were several restaurants. A Tibetan was carrying away cases of empty beer bottles on a pedal rickshaw. Chinese waiters were cleaning a dimly lit restaurant with its shutters still halfway down.

The restaurants alternated with hairdressing salons. A manicurist in black trousers and platform heels was washing her hair out in the open on the three steps that led from the pavement to the entrance of her salon. There was a transistor radio on the ground next to her. It was blaring the latest Hong Kong pop hits.

I passed a young Chinese couple. The man's hair was slick with brillantine. He wore a black suit and tie. The jacket had three buttons and showy lapels. He was talking into a mobile phone.

The woman was dressed all in white. Stiff-brimmed straw hat with a bow. Half-sleeved shirt. Hotpants. Stilettoes. Only her shiny fake leather bag was red.

Further on, I caught up with a young Tibetan monk walking in the opposite direction. His face was emaciated and he wore worn-out shoes. He was with a woman who was still young but had matted grey hair. Her eyes were feverish. She was scavenging intently in the dustbins along the Beijing Zhonglu.

The shops along this stretch of the wide tree-lined avenue were mostly selling mobile phones. The most common brands were 'Chino-e' and 'BBK'.

I came across a young Chinese prostitute. She couldn't have been more than twenty. She was wearing a white sleeveless T-shirt with the words 'I love you' on it in black, in letters of different shapes and sizes. The young woman was wearing an extremely short miniskirt. It showed off a good pair of legs, albeit a bit stiff from too much walking up and down the avenue. As I went by the girl opened her lips slightly, smiled at me and murmured 'Hello.'

The Beijing Zhonglu led to a huge round square. Three large buildings gave on to it. There was the five storey 'Tibet Jinzhu Group' building, the futuristic 'Broadcasting and TV Centre,' Lhasa's television headquarters, and the anonymous 'Lhasa Construction Bank' building with an eye-catching Volkswagen billboard.

The centre of the square held an unusual monument — two enormous gold-plated yaks. The monument had been inaugurated on the 26th May 1991 to mark the fortieth anniversary of the 'liberation' of the Tibetan capital. The gold-plated yaks stood on a wine-red, irregularly shaped base.

The yak on the left appeared to be looking worriedly at the traffic bearing down on it from all directions. The one on the right had its front hooves firmly on the base and stood, chest out and horns pointing skyward, in an appropriately Socialist rhetoric pose.

Under the yak, shielded by a red umbrella, two policemen armed with rifles and binoculars kept an eye on the road leading to the Potala.

Instead of crossing the square and continuing along the Beijing Zhonglu, I turned left at this point to take the Lingkor Xilu, West Lingkor Road, another big tree-lined avenue.

There was a smaller building alongside the 'Tibetan Jinzhu Group' building. It was the Foreign Trade Centre. Immediately after it came the lofty 'Bank of China' building. Two bronze lions crouching on a granite base guarded the staircase leading to the glass and cement building. The lion on the right was roaring angrily, despite being comfortably seated on his rear paws. A middle-aged Tibetan sat at his feet displaying his wares, which were neatly arranged on a grey cloth - bicycle pedals, brakes and chains. From his position on the pavement the man watched the traffic speeding past raptly.

I passed more restaurants and hairdressers and reached a large collection of buildings that hosted the Lhasa Middle School. It had over two thousand students. As in all of Tibet's secondary schools, the medium of instruction was Chinese. There were 120 teachers. Only 30 of them were Tibetan and only seven of these taught Tibetan.

Another imposing building under construction, with cement pillars encased in wooden formwork, marked the end of the Lingkor Xilu.

I turned right at a right angle and walked along a third tree-lined avenue. There was a board that read 'Central Part of North Lingkor Road.'

The shops here were smaller and more modest:

The first shop was selling audiocassettes of Chinese pop music. The next one had second-hand washing machines in pastel shades. The third sold aluminium sheets.

A little further on I reached a side entrance to the 'Liberation Park.' Here too, 'liberation' referred to the military invasion of Tibet by the Chinese in October 1950.

The eastern part of the park was a big fun fair.

There was a miniature train with a red and blue metal dragon on the front of the locomotive.

There was a giant wheel, its hanging seats ready to accommodate courting couples. People's Liberation Army soldiers and Chinese hairdressers were carried higher than the centuries-old trees in the park then came sharply back down to ground level.

There were pagoda-shaped kiosks with green roofs. Brightly coloured cloth umbrellas shielded the tables of an open-air café. The place overlooked a small irregularly shaped lake on which two-seater pedalos were moored, waiting to be hired.

The northern façade of the Potala towered above the entire amusement park. The majestic edifice seemed wounded by all this vulgarity.

At the centre of the 'Liberation Park' was a bigger lake, the lake of the Naga King.

The Naga King was a dragon with a serpent's body. He was the head of the serpent-spirits living in the lake on which the Potala was built. The sixth Dalai Lama came to an agreement with the spirit. In exchange for the serpent's protection of the place he would build a chapel in his honour on the island at the centre of the lake.

I crossed a small arched cement bridge to visit the Lukhang, the little temple dedicated to the Naga King.

The edifice's three stories were brightly painted. The base of the temple was shaped like a mandala. The roof was a squat hexagonal pyramid. A high gold-plated pinnacle topped the building.

The willows on the island had branches so long that they lapped the surface of the lake.

Half a dozen white ducks were resting on one of the branches. There were several others in the lake. They had brown feathers, white necks, bottle green heads and long yellow beaks.

I went inside the little temple. The Naga king's chapel was shabby and bare. I came out again almost immediately.

As I left, when I was already on the small cement bridge, I turned once again towards the Lukhang. I wanted a last glance at the temple of the Spirit of the Lake.

On the first floor of the small building, under a blue and white striped tent, was a very elderly Tibetan monk in a patched-up robe.

He was as pale as a lizard.

He stared at me, standing so still he might have been a ghost.

II

Yesterday.

Spencer Chapman continues his description of the Lingkor.

Having coasted the external wall of the Temple of the Serpent, the sacred way goes through barley fields where the harvest is underway and, at the same time, the soil is being prepared for planting.

Spencer Chapman writes, 'Now they are starting to plough up the fields with yaks and dzos harnessed in pairs. This must be finished before the ground is held by the winter frosts.

'All at once, close at hand, there is a deep booming noise that sets the air a-tremble; it sounds like a hoarse syren or a large animal in dire distress. It is produced by three monks who are sitting on the ground practising on the twelve-foot long monastery pipes. The noise is so great that they have to come out into the fields to practice.'

The Lingkor approaches the city: 'On the left of the road are the hovels of the lowest class of Lhasa society, the Ragyappa, a community of scavenging beggars whose work it is to dispose of the dead bodies. When Buddhists die, their bodies must return to the elements from which they originated — earth, fire, water, air. In the Tibetan winter the ground is frozen too hard for graves to be dug; where yak-dung is the chief fuel not enough can be spared for cremation; many people drink from the river so that if the corpses are consigned to water the drinking supply would be contaminated. So the body returns to the air. The Ragyappa may be seen in the early morning carrying on their backs the huddled corpses of the poor. These grisly burdens are taken to appointed places where they are laid out on flat stones and cut into small pieces. These are thrown to the vultures and ravens who crowd round waiting for their share of the loathsome meal. These Ragyappa must also remove the carcasses of animals that die in the city. Another of their duties is to seek out thieves and robbers who flee from the city to the surrounding country.'

But not all the Ragyappa are poor, Spencer Chapman tells us. 'Some of the Ragyappa are very wealthy and wear the saucer-shaped hat and earring of respectability.'

From this viewpoint the Ramoche temple is visible in the distance.

'On the right, close to the Lingkor, appears the single golden roof-pavilion of the Ramoche temple, in which is a huge image of the Chinese wife of King Songsten Gampo. Opposite this temple a road from Sera monastery and the arsenal comes in from the left. Already a line of bare-headed, bare-footed monks are entering the city; many of them carry on their backs bundles wrapped up in a flap of their voluminous robes.'

After crossing the north-eastern corner of the city the Lingkor reaches the butchers quarter. 'The ground is littered with horns, hoofs, bones and scraps of hide. Inappropriately placed among the slaughterhouses and butcheries is the mosque of the Ladakis, rather a mean and neglected-looking building with a wooden lich gate and enclosing wall. The main road from north Tibet, Ganden, and Nagchuka comes in here, and beside it is a small walled pagoda in Chinese style. This is the grave of a member of General Huang-Mu Sung's 1932 Mission to Lhasa who died after being thrown from his horse.'

Today.

I left the 'Liberation Park' from the main gate.

An old Tibetan was sitting on the ground in front of the big gate. He was turning a prayer wheel with his right hand. In a faint voice he whispered the mantra 'Om mani padme hum.'

Sonam, the tourist guide with me, gave him a two-yuan note. 'We Tibetans always give alms,' he told me. 'The Chinese never do it. That's why they're such good businessmen.'

I came to a crossroads where the Lingkor Beilu met the Nyangrden Lu. There was another big gold-plated statue at the centre. This one, too, was in line with the strictest standards of Socialist realism.

It was a statue of an archer on a horse, in the act of letting fly an arrow. The horse was impressively muscled. Its front hooves were raised off the ground. Its muzzle was stretched towards a radiant future.

I carried on along the Lingkor Beilu.

Almost all the little shops on the pavement on the right were selling building material. Metal and plastic tubes. Glue and strips of wood. Cans of 'Yang Ming' brand paint. Water pumps. Glass panes.

In front of a sanitary goods shop I saw my first pilgrim measuring his length around the Lingkor.

At first I thought the man (long hair gathered into thin braids, wearing necklaces and colourful clothes) was a nomad. He wore a tattered purple apron to protect his clothes. His hands were bandaged. He prostrated himself repeatedly in the direction of a small shop selling pea green, canary yellow and dusty pink sinks and toilets.

Sonam, my guide, explained that there had been a sacred building on that spot (or in that direction) many years previously. It had been swept away by the New Lhasa master plan.

Two elegant Chinese women approached from the opposite direction. They were very beautiful. They had long legs in tight-fitting black trousers. They wore silk shirts — one wine red, the other sea green. The red shirt had antique Chinese characters on it in filigree that sparkled gold each time the woman moved.

When the two women caught sight of the man on the pavement they got a fright. They clutched each other and looked at the prostrate man in horror.

I passed the 'People's Hospital of the Autonomous Region of Tibet.' I reached the point at which the Lingkor Beilu gave way to the Ramoche Lu, the road that led to the Ramoche Temple buildings.

King Songsten Gampo's Chinese wife built the temple in the seventh century. It was here that the statue of Jowo Shakyamuni had originally been placed. During the Cultural Revolution the entire complex had been destroyed. In 1985 the Chinese re-opened the temple for prayer. But when I visited it fifteen years later, many of the buildings were still in ruins.

The stretch of the Beijing Beilu I was on ended at a three-storeyed building covered in the usual shiny white tiles. Several armed policemen guarded it. There was a high pylon wire on the top with a telegraph antenna. The front of the building had ten columns in chrome metal. It was decorated with chains of red flags. The sign was written in Chinese and English: 'Telecommunications Building.'

The post office faced a huge round square. There were other big buildings — the Silver Bridge Hotel, the Hotel Plateau in 'neo-Tibetan' style, the headquarters of the Bank of China.

At the centre of the square was the third monument of the 'new' Lingkor. This time the design was decidedly Soviet. There were four squat grey stone figures in overalls and aviator glasses. They had a big flag with the five stars of the People's Republic of China, also made of grey stone, hoisted onto their shoulders. If the effort on the faces of the four was anything to go by, the flag weighed a ton.

Five roads led off the big circle like spokes. The Lingkor Beilu, the road I had just walked down. The Togde Lu, which led to the famous Drapchi prison. The Nagachen Lu, leading to the Gutsa and Lhundrub prisons. The Dagiao Lu, leading to the Lhasa Bridge over the Kyichu river. Finally, there was the Lingkor Donglu, East Lingkor Road, the continuation of what was once the 'sacred way' of Lhasa.

I took this last road.

There were many shops on the ground floor of the imposing Bank of China building.

The usual mobile phone shops and hairdressers. I counted thirty-seven different mobile phone models in one window.

The Chinese hairdressers and manicurists were wearing microscopic miniskirts. Perched on high metal stools, they waited for customers, their legs crossed.

The other side of the Lingkor Donglu ran along the old town. All the existing buildings had been destroyed and rebuilt in 'neo-Tibetan style'. The main structure was made of concrete. The walls were made of small, prefabricated concrete blocks. The doors and windows had metal frames. In addition, large black frames painted on the wall surface ran around the windows to maintain the 'local features'.

The destruction of the old section of Lhasa was decided right from the first master plan.

The drawing up of the plan started in 1959 and was only completed in 1980. That year, with the Central Committee's *Document Number 31*, the Chinese Communist Party entrusted urban planners with the task of making Lhasa a 'rich, civilised and clean city.'

The Beijing government approved the master plan in 1984 and the bulldozers arrived in the Tibetan capital almost immediately after.

The old town was disembowelled. The buildings in front of the Jokhang were knocked down to make place for a large square.

In 1993, a big banner appeared in Barkor Square. It said, in Tibetan: 'Beggars and unemployed persons will no longer be allowed to live in the Barkor. We will carry our project forward day after day. We will make the city of Lhasa even more beautiful.'

Hundreds of houses were razed to the ground. In their place, anonymous buildings with 'local features' came up - a caricature of the Tibetan architecture they replaced.

I reached the intersection with the Beijing Donglu, the big road that crossed the entire city.

Seated on the pavement of East Beijing Road were Tibetan men and women selling broomcorn, potatoes, apples, barley, spices and brass bells to tie around sheep and goats' necks.

I had to enter the old city in order to walk the brief stretch of Lingkor Nanlu, the Lingkor's southern part.

Lingkor South was a narrow road adjoining the Barkor area. The pavement was lined with the dirty curtains that covered the entry of small Tibetan shops. There was a baker's, a barber shop and a restaurant serving thupka and steamed momos.

There was a small mosque at the end of the road. It looked as if it were made of papier mâché. It had an onion-shaped dome and a short minaret with vertical white and green stripes. The minaret ended in a mini-dome rising to a point on which a lopsided tin half-moon had been fixed.

The road in front of the mosque was paved with hexagonal blocks of porphyry.

There were Muslim salesmen seated on the ground. They had slanting eyes and sparse beards. They wore white skull caps on their heads and were selling cauliflower, potatoes and onions.

III

Yesterday.

The Lingkor now turns westwards and finds an opening between the Kyichu river and the city. There are piles of garbage and stacks of firewood. Spencer Chapman passes a section of the old town walls.

The sacred way runs along willow groves, a waterfall and then the Kyichu river, which clings to the road at this point.

The most difficult and most beautiful stretch of the Lingkor begins.

Spencer Chapman writes, 'And now, before completing the circuit, we must cross the precipitous south-western Buttresses of the Iron Hill. It is impossible to keep on the level, because a stream washes right against the foot of the rocks. So the path, with steep crags above and below, cuts over the shoulder of the hill. This is perhaps the most remarkable part of the whole Lingkor. Beside the track are hundreds and hundreds of carved and painted Buddhas. Some are cut out of the rock itself. Others are painted on flat slates and propped up in niches. There are also the horns of animals and innumerable clay castings of the Buddha, which are baked in a primitive kiln beside the track. The Lingkor here descends so steeply that those measuring their length may cease their uncomfortable progress and walk to the foot of the hill. On the right are three large prayer barrels built into the wall, these must be turned as you pass. A little farther on is a vertical wall of smooth rock, on which are painted several hundred similar Buddhas in red, blue, and gold. They are arranged in ranks both vertically and horizontally. Just below the multiple wall painting is a rock which must be touched with the forehead. It is polished to the smoothness of marble. There is also a small hole in the wall forming the summit of a painted chorten; a finger must be placed here. Another devotional exercise is to crawl under a slab of rock that leans against the foot of the main wall. These actions, especially the last two, are often dispensed with. From the top of the wall long strings of prayer flags are stretched above the Lingkor to the trees beside the stream. One more chorten is passed and the Sacred Way runs between two willow groves to the Norbu Lingka gate where we first entered it.'

Today.

I left the noise and smells of the old town behind me and emerged onto a huge, deserted road — the Jin Zhu Donglu. Its pavements were over eight metres wide. They were paved with prefabricated yellow, green and red bricks.

The road was extremely wide and perfectly straight. It had a vanishing point to infinity.

Squeezed between the road and a bend in the Kyichu river was the People's Liberation Army military command headquarters.

The complex in which it was situated was as big as the entire old town of Lhasa. Between the boundary wall of the headquarters and the Jin Zhu Donglu was a long line of low two storied buildings. They held a few shops and several brothels.

Faded curtains were drawn over the doors of the brothels. Through the open curtains at the windows I could see Chinese prostitutes sitting on worn velvet couches. Some were standing on their doorsteps waiting for customers. The more elegant prostitutes were dressed in white. They wore semi-transparent tight silk dresses. The dresses came down to their ankles and showed glimpses of the women's bras and panties.

On the other pavement a few Tibetan pilgrims were walking along the Lingkor.

I passed an old lady with grey hair and a cream coloured cloth cap. She had a black umbrella tied to her bent back.

I came up alongside a man holding the hands of two young women wearing black chubas. They walked along the sacred way chanting mantras.

I passed another old lady. She had a cloth bag over her shoulder and was spinning her prayer wheel. She held a string with which she was leading a small Tibetan dog in her left hand. Another dog without a leash, with a bell around its neck, followed her.

I was now walking down a stretch of the large road known as the Jin Zhu Zhonglu. On the left was a big hotel, the Kel Sa Yun Hotel, all glass and concrete. There was the red five-star flag of the People's Republic of China in the round entrance pavilion.

A section of the Kyichu river lapped against the road. A row of tall weeping willows shielded the water from view. In the background the silvery mountains of the Lhasa valley could be seen.

A concrete bridge led to the 'National City of Chonghe.' The area emerged between two sections of the Kyichu river. It was also called the 'City of Fun.' It had low buildings with sloping roofs.

There were neon signs on the roofs — KTV ('Karaoke TV'), or the Chinese characters KA and LA followed by the letters OK (Karaoke).

By day the city was deserted. It came alive by night.

In the 'National City' the People's Liberation Army soldiers could get drunk on beer and have sex with prostitutes.

An unofficial 1998 survey revealed that there were 658 brothels and 238 'dance halls' and 'karaoke bars' where prostitution was common in the eighteen main streets of Lhasa.

The number of brothels went up to over one thousand if the entire city were taken into account. To these would have to be added the hundreds of 'karaoke bars' where young women offered their services on the upper floor.

Walking down the Jin Zhu Zhonglu, I reached the foot of the Chakpo Ri.

A very tall antenna topped the 'Iron Hill'.

The guide indicated a dirt lane. It ran between two walls that were over four metres high.

At the beginning of the little road was a heap of flat, round stones. The ones on top had been given a coat of whitewash.

At the other end of the lane was a tree covered with prayer flags.

There were also ropes on the sides of the hill with thousands of coloured flags hung on them.

I began climbing along the slope of the Chakpo Ri.

The section that F. Spencer Chapman had called 'the most beautiful part of the entire Lingkor' was starting. But I wasn't expecting much. I was convinced by now that Lhasa's 'sacred way' didn't exist any more.

The lane had become a narrow path.

There was a long stretch of rocks painted granite red.

There were hundreds of little pictures of the Buddha painted in bright colours.

There were two yak's horns. 'Om mani padme hum' was written in Tibetan on the fragment of skull that held the horns together. The same mantra had been carved into hundreds of flat, round stones.

There was barleycorn scattered in front of the holy pictures.

There were also cans of beer and Sprite with water in them, as votive offerings.

I had climbed to over thirty metres above road level. I looked back. I saw the Iron Hill besieged by a vast quarter of anonymous concrete parallelepipeds. It was the headquarters of the People's Armed Police.

A red flag fluttered in a small square between the monotonous white barracks. The insistent notes of a military march emerged from a loudspeaker.

I started climbing again.

I could hear a concerted beating of chisels on stone.

Under a tin roof three Tibetan stonecutters were carving the 'Om mani padme hum' mantra on tens of mani-stones. I bought one for five yuan. I would take it to India and deposit it on the little Lingkor in McLeod Ganj.

I went on climbing the narrow path strewn with sharp stones.

Taking a hairpin bend, I found myself in front of an entire painted stretch of the Iron Hill.

It was a spectacular and unexpected image.

'It's a miracle,' I thought.

No one had managed to destroy this wall of the Chakpo Ri.

The Chinese bombings of 1959 hadn't managed it.

The long years of the Cultural Revolution, when the 'Om mani padme hum' mantra had been replaced by 'Mao Zedong wan sui[1],' hadn't managed it.

'Lha gyalo,' 'Victory to the gods,' whispered Sonam, my Tibetan guide.

In the centre of the wall was a big picture of the Buddha Shakyamuni. The Buddha's face, shoulders, right arm and left hand were painted in a blue so deep as to seem black. His stark-white eyes were like headlamps at night.

Alongside the Buddha were thousands of other figures, large and small. The predominant colours were red, white, green blue and orange.

A few elderly Tibetans had prostrated themselves in front of the large painting.

There were two sleeping dogs, one black, the other white and brown.

I passed the devout making their obeisance. An old Tibetan lady smiled at me.

The small dirt road, crushed between two whitewashed walls, now began to descend slightly.

About fifty metres on I reached Norbulingka Lu at the exact

---

1. 'Mao Zedong will live 10,000 years'.

spot at which I had begun my walk.

It had taken me three hours and twelve minutes to complete my tour of the Lingkor.

***

That evening I had a dinner meeting with my 'contact.' It was Tenzin, a friend who lived in the refugee camp of Majnu ka Tilla in Delhi, who had found me my 'contact.' I was to meet him in a Tibetan restaurant on the first floor of a building in Old Lhasa.

The restaurant had two entrances. Coming in through the side entrance, I had to go through a dark corridor and courtyard, then pass a dirty, smoke-filled kitchen. A set of steep stairs led to the first floor.

The food was served in a room with wooden tables and benches. The principal Tibetan monuments had been painted directly onto the wall in oils. The paintings were splotchy and crude.

There was a group of young Western tourists in the restaurant. They were discussing the dollar-yuan exchange rate animatedly.

I sat down at a table by myself. The sound of traffic in the road below came in through the windows. A shapely, courteous Tibetan woman came to take my order. I told her I was waiting for someone.

My 'contact' arrived at seven on the dot. He identified me immediately. 'Hi,' he said. We ordered two thupkas, a soup with noodles and chunks of meat and vegetables.

The Tibetan sitting in front of me was young. He had an open, friendly face. He wore a shapeless grey outfit. He did temporary jobs to get by. I told him about my tour of the Lingkor that morning.

'Soon the Chinese will wipe out our culture forever,' he said. 'We can't compete with them. Today, the only thing that matters in Lhasa is making money. If you want a good job your mother tongue has to be Chinese. If you want to start any sort of business you need to have money, the right contacts and preferably a Chinese Communist Party badge in your pocket. We've become second-class citizens in our own country. We don't count for anything any more. Here in Lhasa, the Chinese have opened karaoke bars, gaming rooms and discos everywhere. All that's left for us young Tibetans is drinking, gambling and whoring.'

The conversation was painful and went on for a long time. The soup was mediocre. And anyway it had gone cold.

***

McLeod Ganj (India).

On the way down from McLeod Ganj, Temple Road led to the foot of a small hill with a round base. On the hill were the Central Cathedral, the Institute of Buddhist Dialectics, the Namgyal monastery and, at the very top, the Dalai Lama's residence.

The Lingkor of McLeod Ganj circled this little hill.

There was a big iron garbage crate in front of the Institute of Buddhist Dialectics.

Over the crate was a big hand-painted poster. On the right were side views of a buffalo, a cow, a yak, a goat, a sheep and a pig. On the left, standing in a pond with their feet in the water, were a rooster and a duck. In English and Tibetan the poster said:

TAKE PITY ON ANIMALS
DO NOT CAUSE THEIR SLAUGHTER
BE A VEGETARIAN.

For a brief stretch the Lingkor of McLeod Ganj met the asphalt road that led to the Library.

After the second curve I left the main road. A small cement bridge crossed a smelly rivulet. A group of macaques with copper coloured fur and some crows were fighting noisily over a rubbish heap.

The sacred way was now a tongue of asphalt just over a metre wide.

Along the path were small heaps of polished, white-painted stones. I placed the mani-stone I had brought from Lhasa on top of one of these piles.

'Om mani padme hum,' I murmured automatically, lost in thought.

The valley of Dharamsala opened out below me on my left. A range of high, pale blue mountains formed the backdrop of the valley.

Large falcons glided effortlessly, their wings wide open.

There were faraway voices from the valley floor.

To the right of the Lingkor the side of the hill rose steeply.

Among the pines, Himalayan oaks and rhododendrons were kennel-type hovels. They barely held one crouching man. One of the old ascetics who lived in these hovels watched me pass. He didn't move. He looked all shrivelled up.

There were coloured boulders along the Lingkor with the 'Om mani padme hum' mantra carved on them. One syllable for each boulder. One colour for each syllable.

A branch of a small knotted oak tree spread horizontally over the path, forming a natural arch. My head brushed it as I passed.

There was an old age home for Tibetans. A few old people were praying under a corrugated tin roof.

Facing them was the boundary wall and the pavilions of a large Buddhist temple. Nagahara, a Japanese architect who had been living in McLeod Ganj for several years, had designed the temple. There were over one hundred prayer barrels on the temple's outer wall.

It was a symmetrical complex. There was a central staircase with two metal poles covered in green cloth at its base. Halfway up the staircase, the flag of independent Tibet fluttered on a white-painted pole. On either side of the flag were two large 'sangkangs', bottle-shaped incense burners. There were also two stupas, their bas-reliefs painted in gold purpurin. There were three small pavilions at the top of the staircase, painted in lively colours. The central pavilion was higher than the other two and was covered by a pagoda roof.

Behind the pavilions the entire side of the hill was hidden under thousands of flags of coloured cloth. They were hung on ropes tied to long bamboo poles.

A light breeze moved the coloured flags that spread the Tibetan mantras in the air.

A black marble slab on the temple's boundary wall read:

> MR. LAWANG NORBU, A DESCENDANT OF
> MARKAM RITSA KHUM,
> BORN IN SHIGATSE AND WIFE MRS. LHAMO
> BORE ALL THE EXPENSES
> AND BUILT 101 HAND SPURRED MANI WHEELS
> CONTAINING 560 MILLION MANI MANTRAS
> IN THE EASTERN PART OF LHAGYAL RI, DHARAMSALA.
> THE COST OF CONSTRUCTION: RS. 275,553.

Beyond the temple complex the Lingkor began to climb.

On the sides of the road the dark, knotted branches of a few oaks stood out against the sky, looking like an old man's hands held out in supplication.

A man was selling tea, biscuits and paan sachets in a wooden lean-to.

I reached the boundary wall of the Dalai Lama's residence. The wall was made of square blocks of grey stone.

An Indian soldier was on guard.

Beyond the wall I could hear the pine trees rustle. I passed a pack of langur monkeys. They had black faces and long grey tails.

Two elderly Tibetan women propped their walking sticks against the boundary wall of the Dalai Lama's residence. They joined their hands respectfully. Then they touched their foreheads to the blocks of grey stone and murmured a few mantras. They began walking once more. I followed a short distance behind them.

The two old women had grey hair and wore dusty chubas. They swayed as they walked. They had well-worn tennis shoes on their feet. Each held a walking stick in her right hand and told the beads on her rosary with the left.

I went past the 'Namgyal Café & Guest House'.

I skirted the exterior wall of the Institute of Buddhist Dialectics.

I had returned to my point of departure.

The Lingkor of McLeod Ganj was over.

But the two elderly Tibetan women didn't stop.

They began another tour of the sacred way. I decided to follow them.

This time I would pray too, in my own way.

I thought of the Tibetans, in exile now for over forty years.

I thought of my thirty-year pilgrimage in the East.

I thought of the impermanence of all things.

Once again I saw the branch that formed an arch over the path.

It started raining — a cold, persistent rain.

I sought refuge under the tin roof in front of the temple designed by the Japanese architect.

A haiku by Basho came to mind:

'From now on
A nameless traveller;
Winter's first rain.'

Select Bibliography

The Tenth of March

Avedon, John F. *The Revolt in Tibet*. New York, 1960.
Barber, Noel. *From the Land of Lost Content*. London, 1969.
Dalai Lama. *My Land and My People*. New York, 1985.
Moraes, Frank. *The Revolt in Tibet*. New York, 1960.
Shakya, Tsering. *The Dragon in the Land of Snow*. London, 1999.

Refugees

Tibet under Chinese Communist Rule. Dharamsala, 1976.

Lobsang Dolma

Dolma, Lobsang. *Lectures on Tibetan Medicine*. Dharamsala, 1986.

Tsering, Tashi, and K. Dondup. *Dolma and Dolkar: Mother and Daughter of Tibetan Medicine*. New Delhi, 1990.

Gu-Chu-Sum

Kerr, Blake. *Sky Burial*. New York, 1997.

Schwartz, Ronald D. *Circle of Protest. Political Ritual in the Tibetan Uprising*. London, 1994.

Panchen Rinpoche

Hilton, Isabel. *The Search for the Panchen Lama*. London, 1999.

Dorje Shugden

Nebesky-Wojkowitz, Réné de. *Oracles and Demons of Tibet*.

The Hague, 1956.
   The Worship of Shugden. Dharamsala.

Karmapa

Maheshwari, Anil. *The Buddha Cries! The Karn Conundrum*. New Delhi, 2000.
   http://www.kagyu.org/karmapa and Karma Triy Dharamchakra.

Lingkor

Chapman, F. Spencer. *Lhasa, the Holy City*. London,